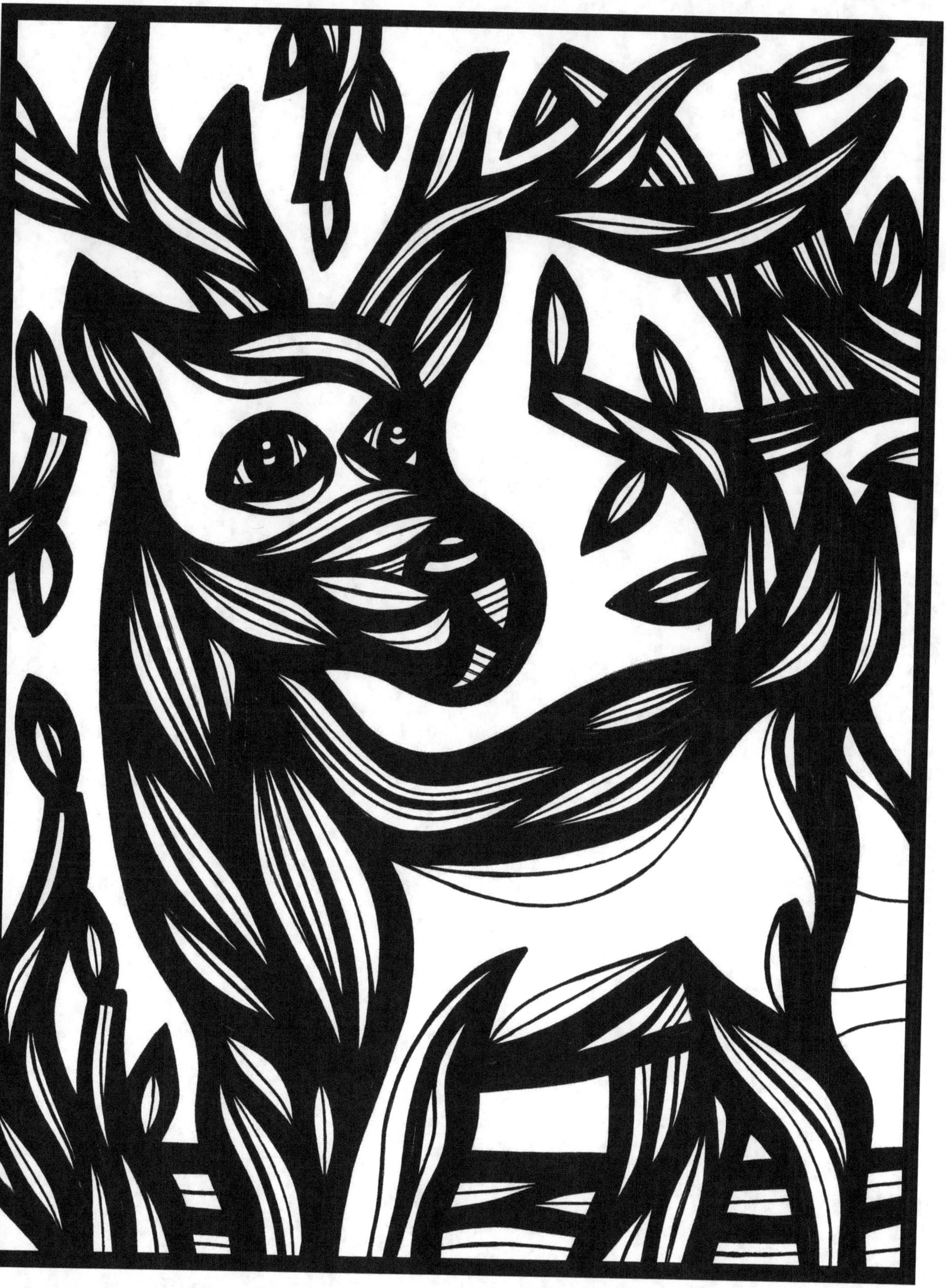

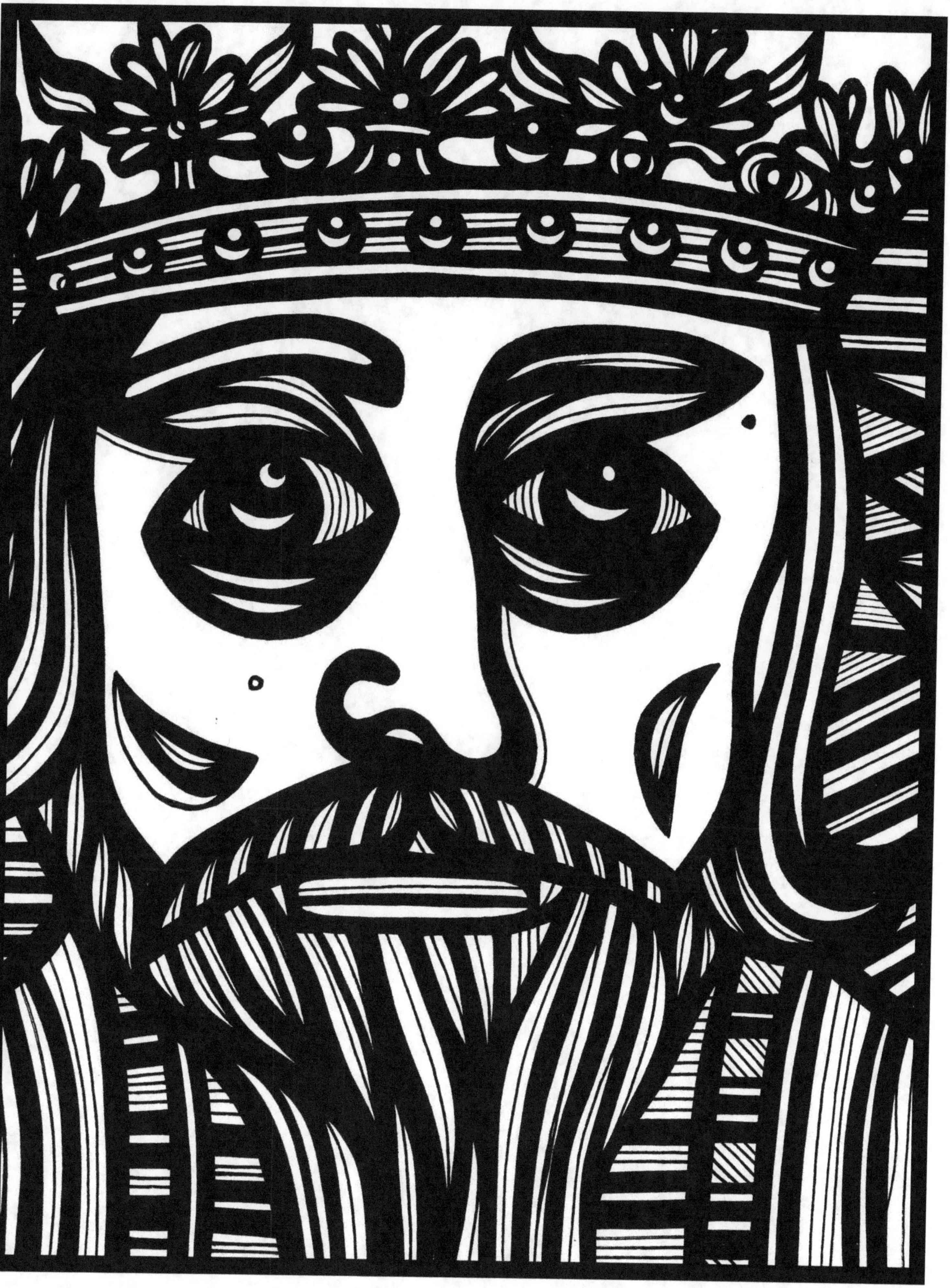

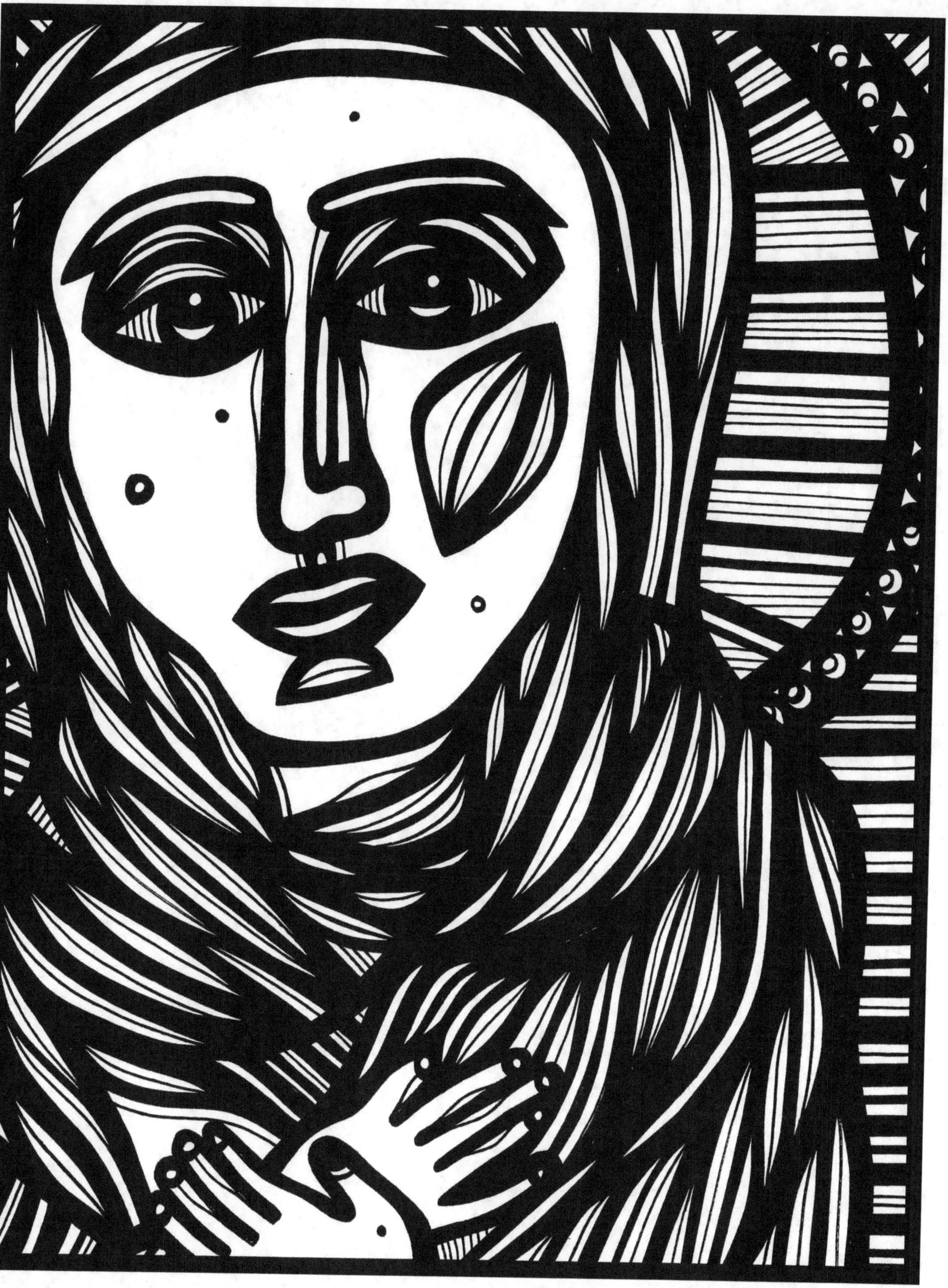

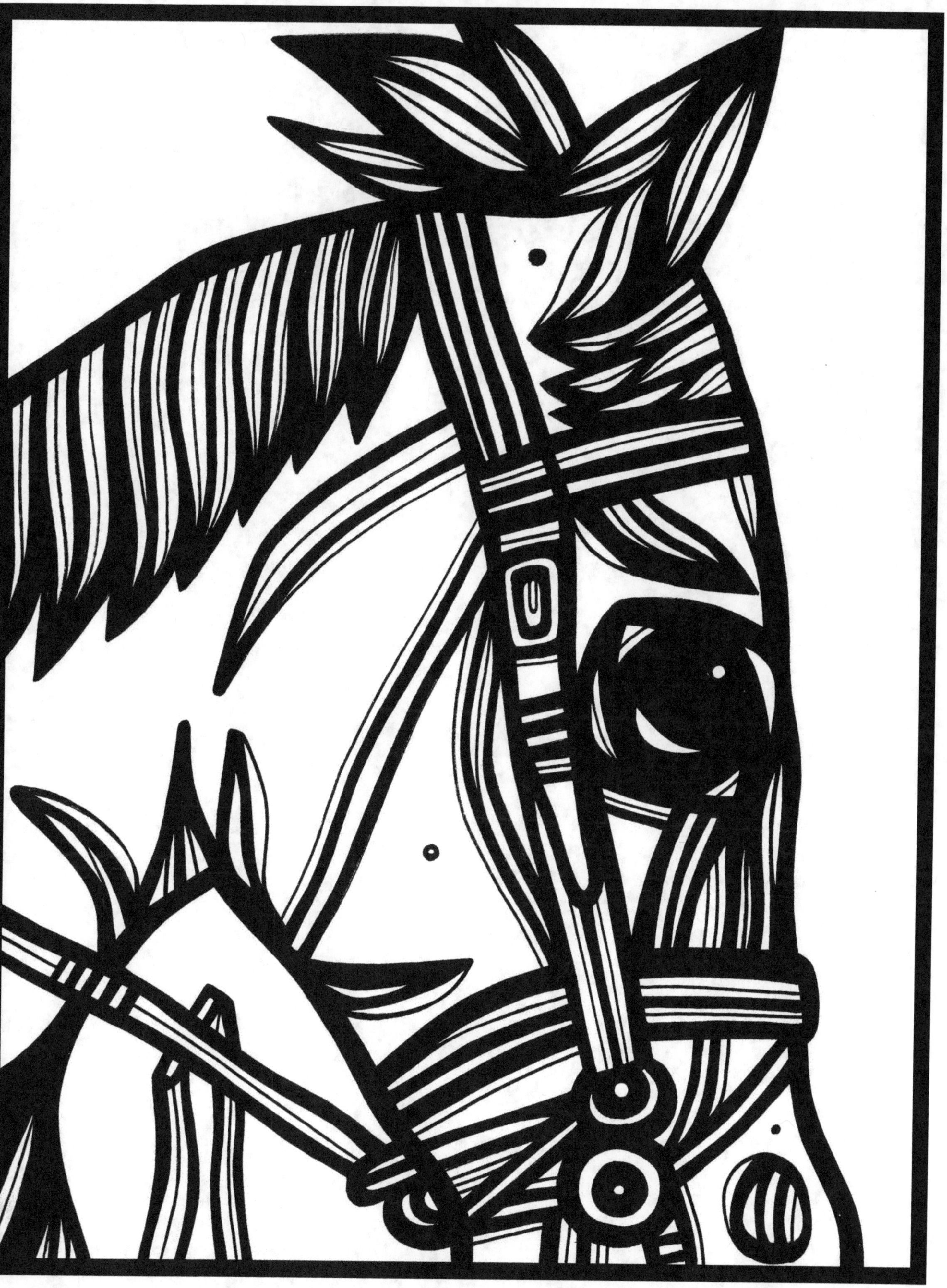

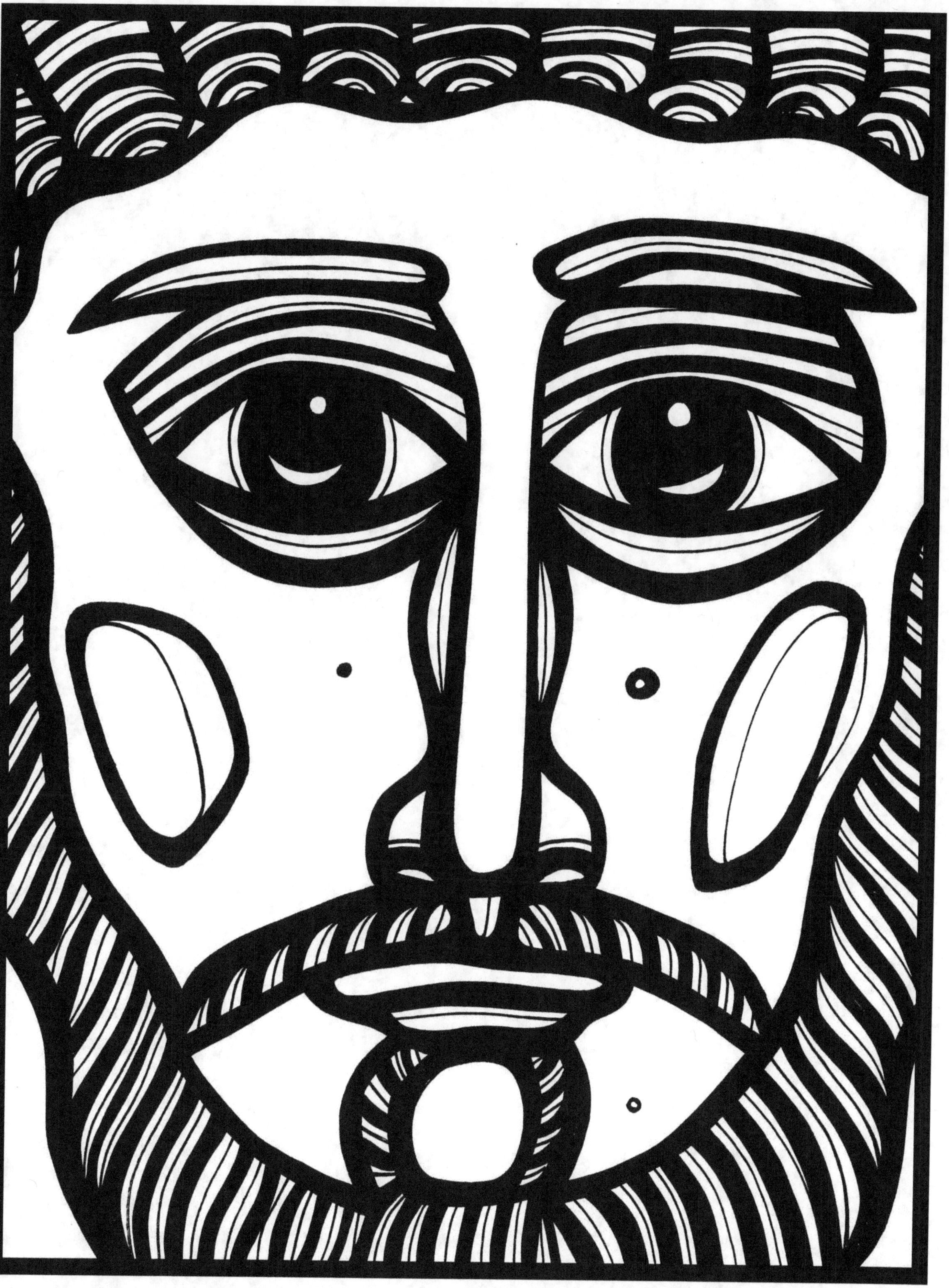

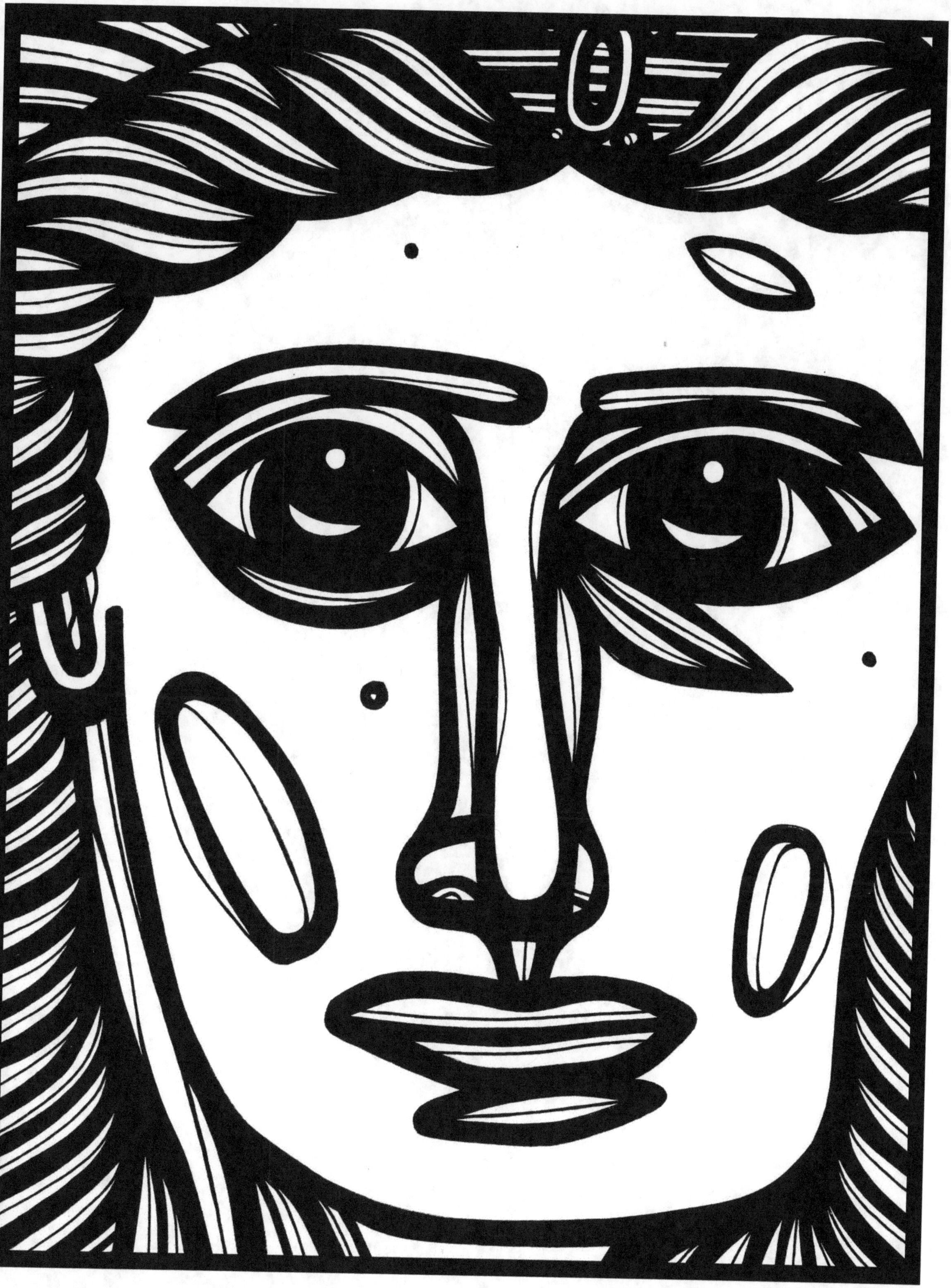

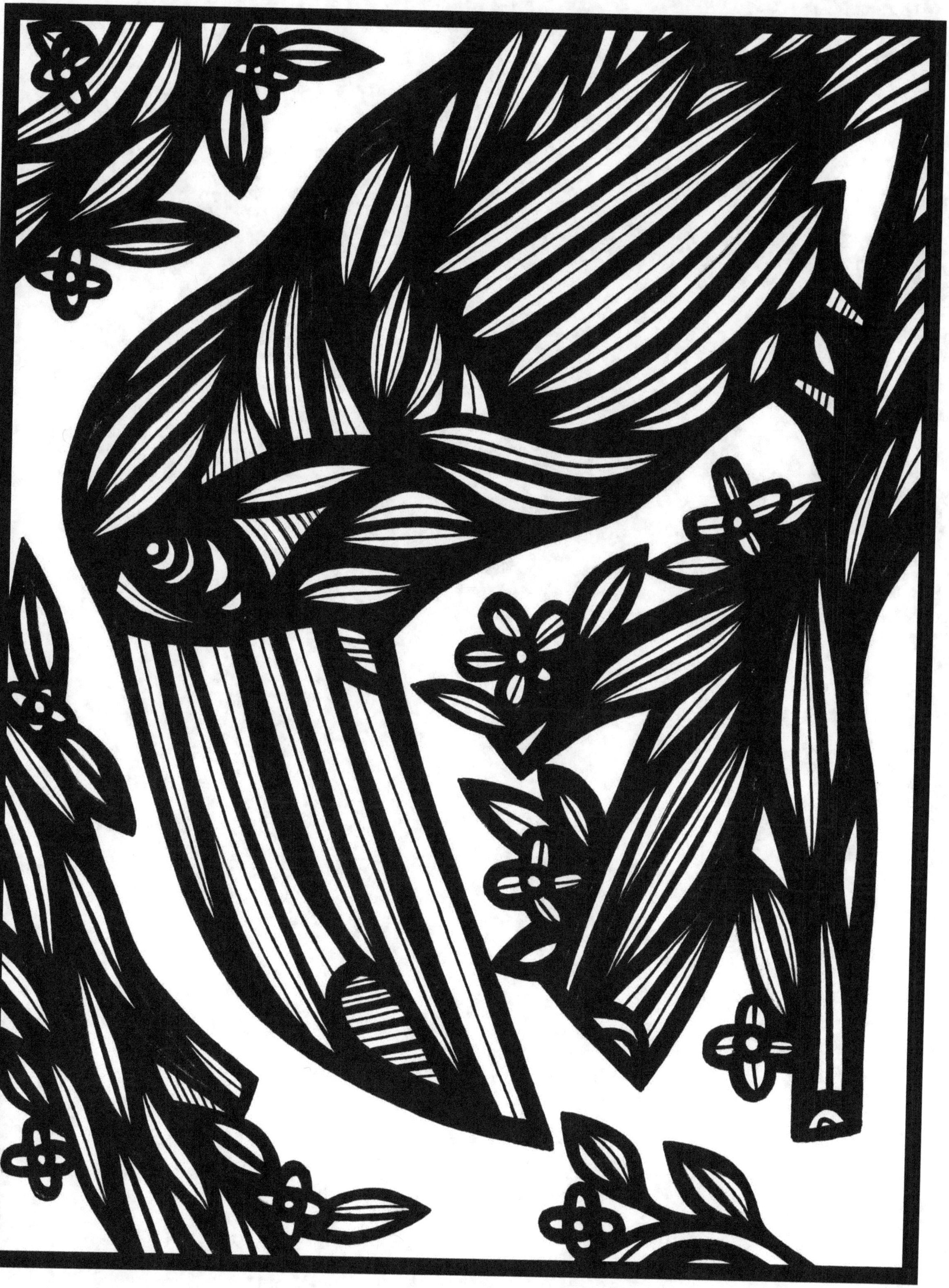

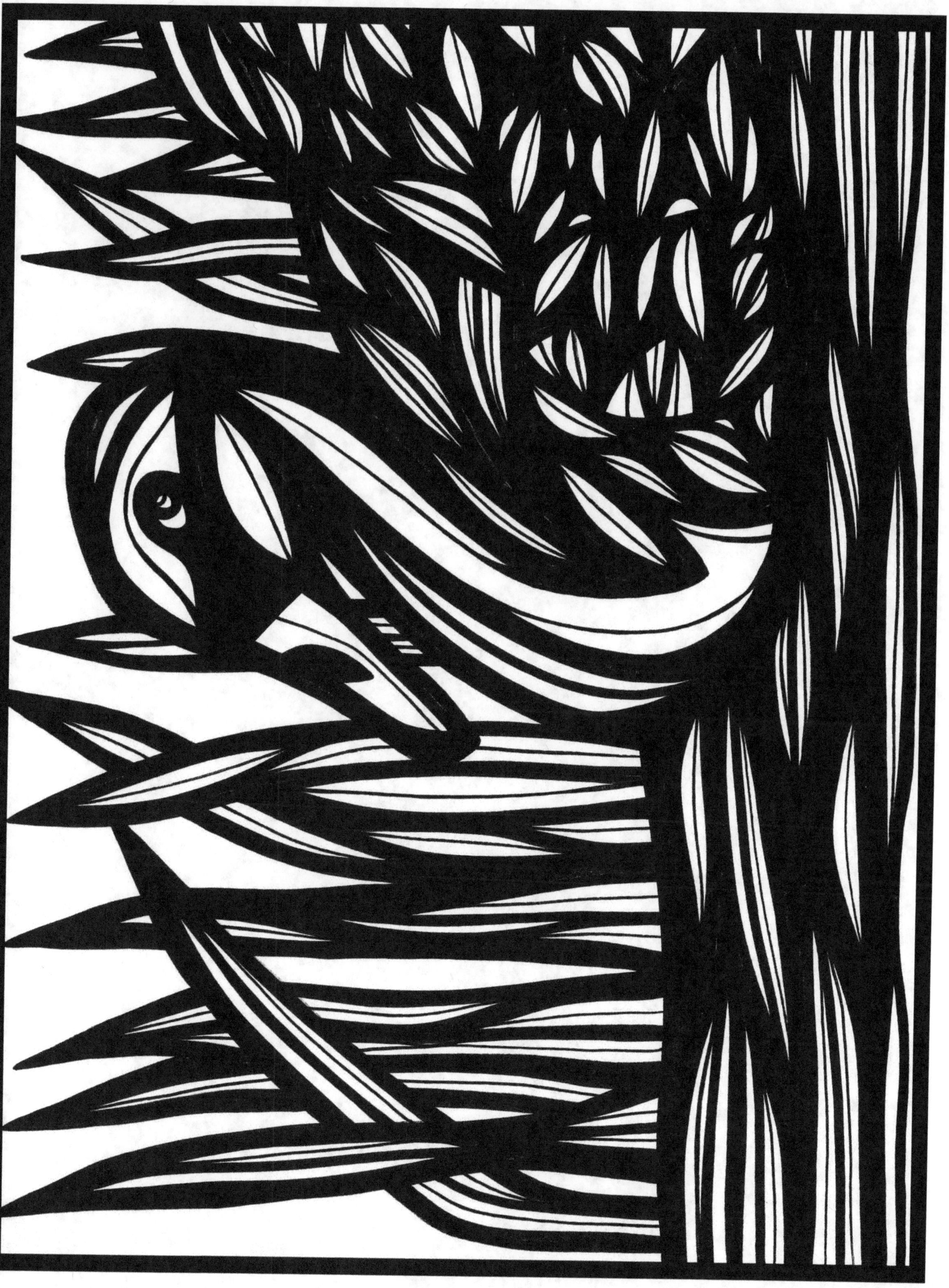

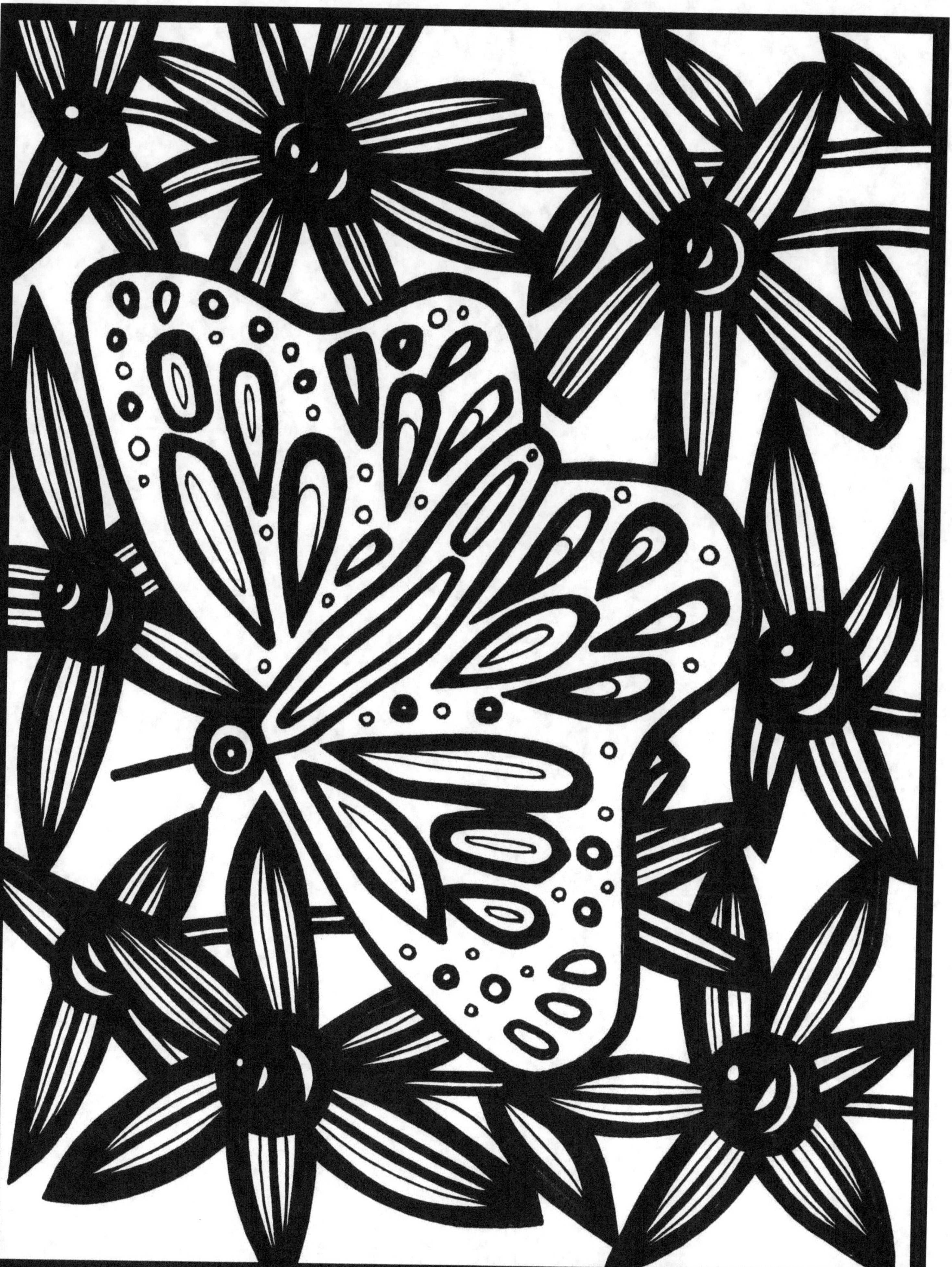

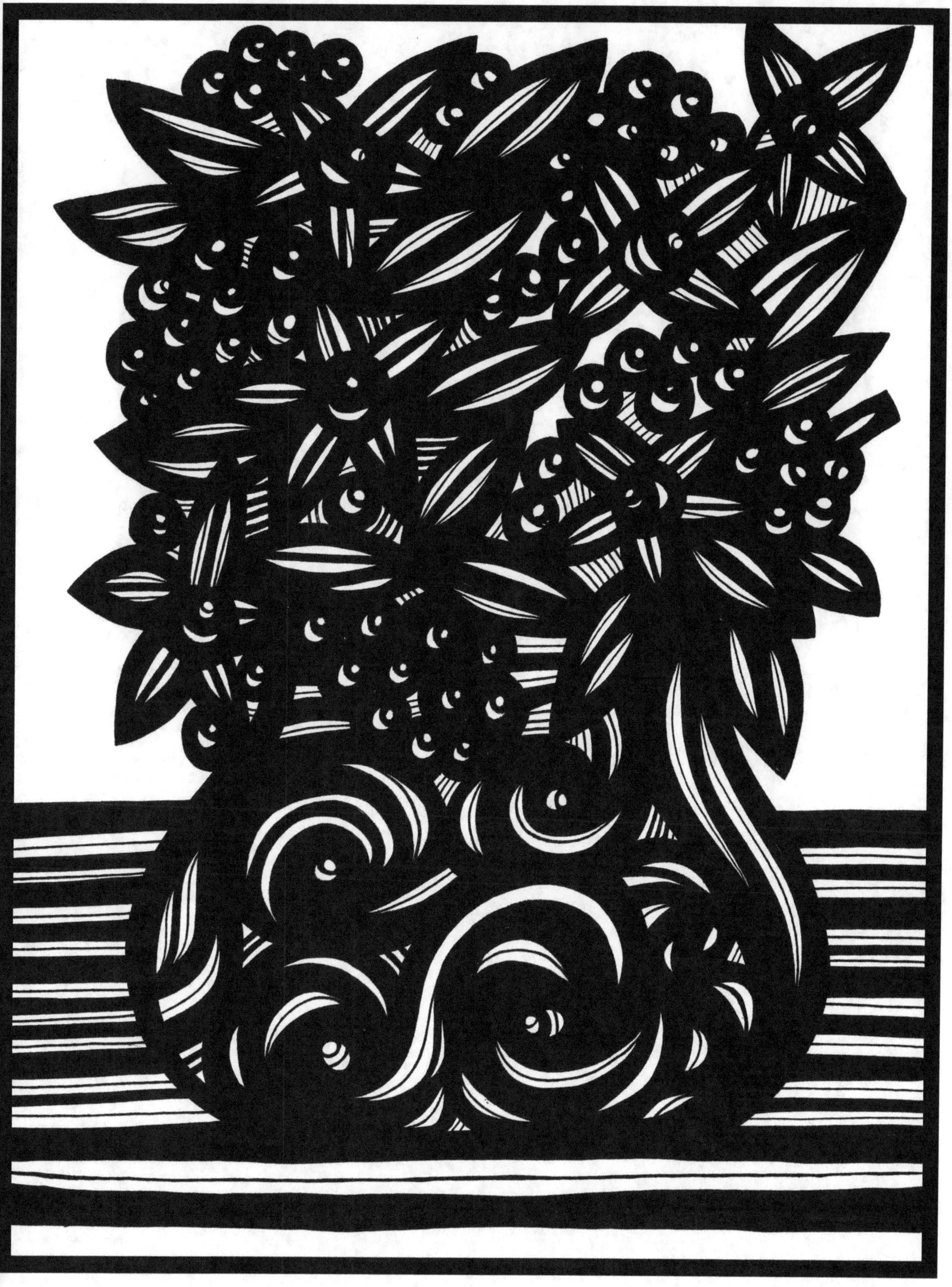

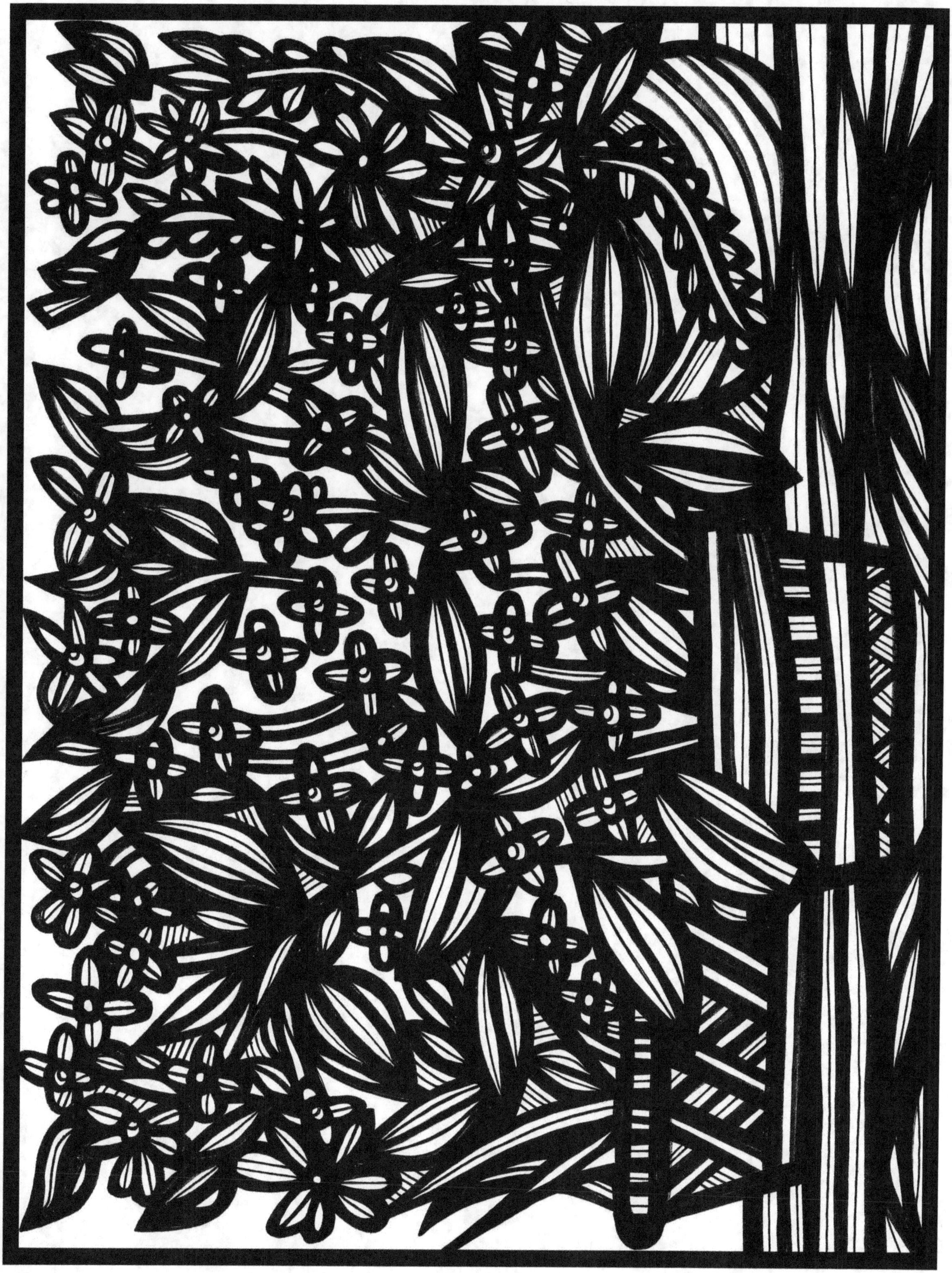

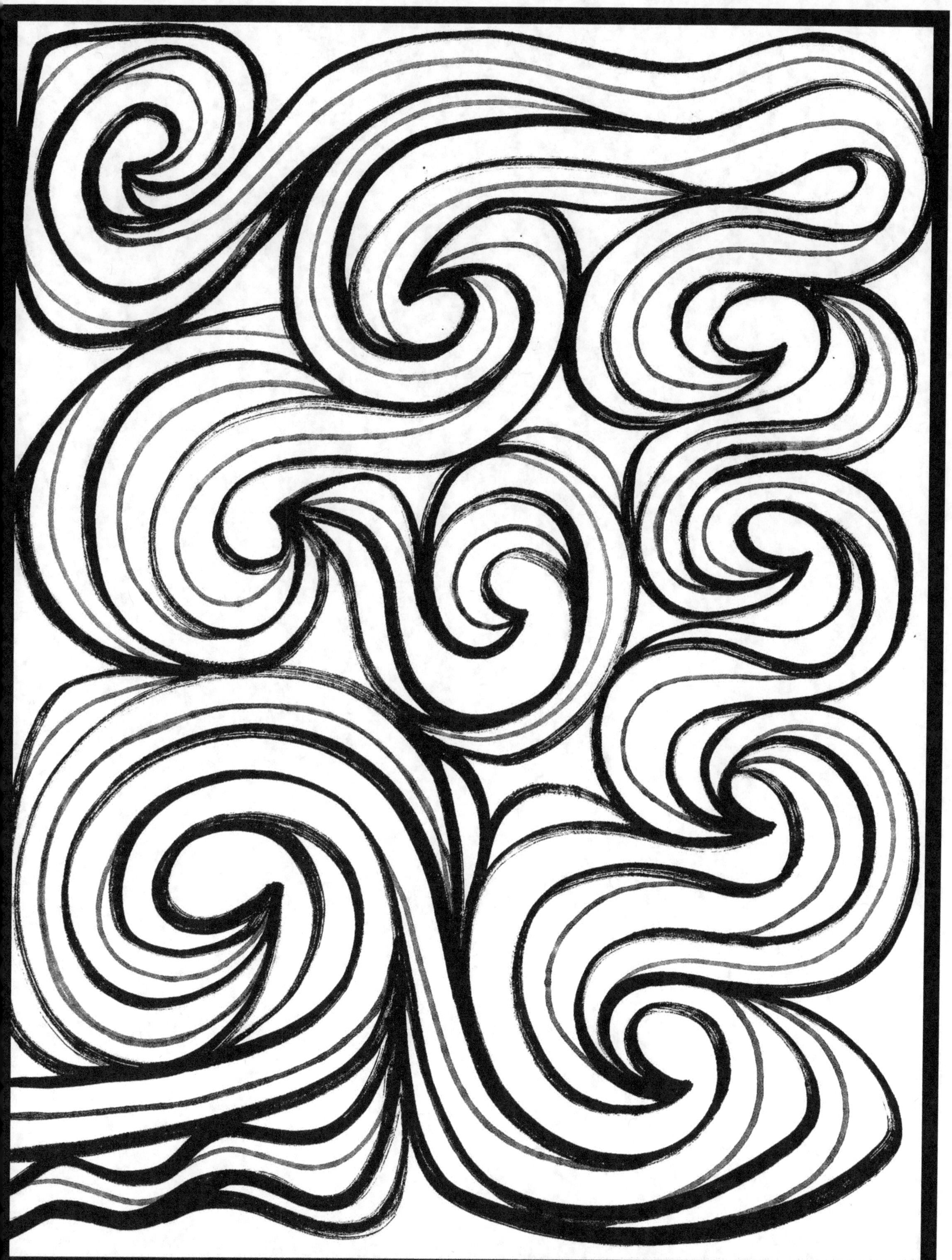

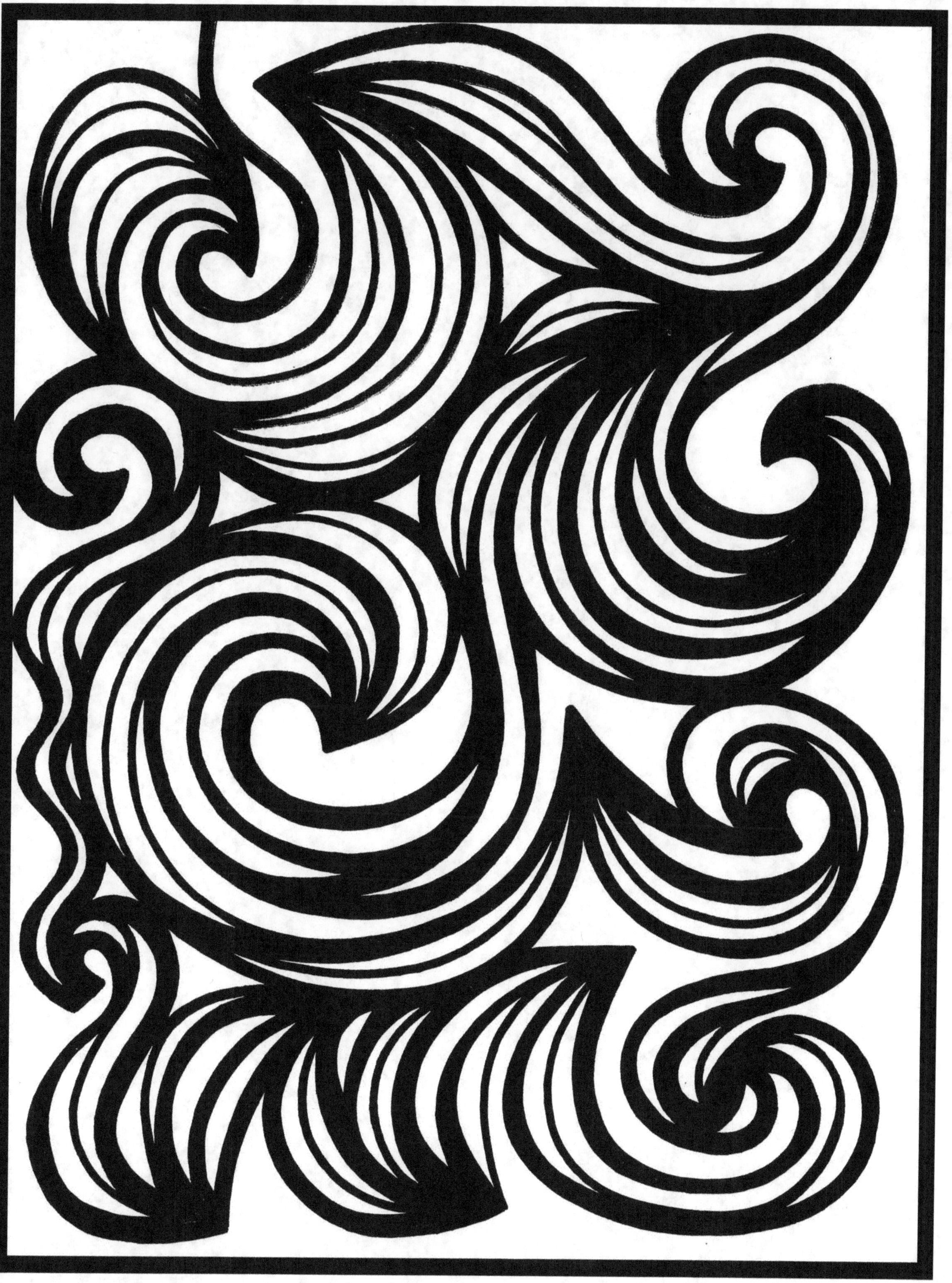

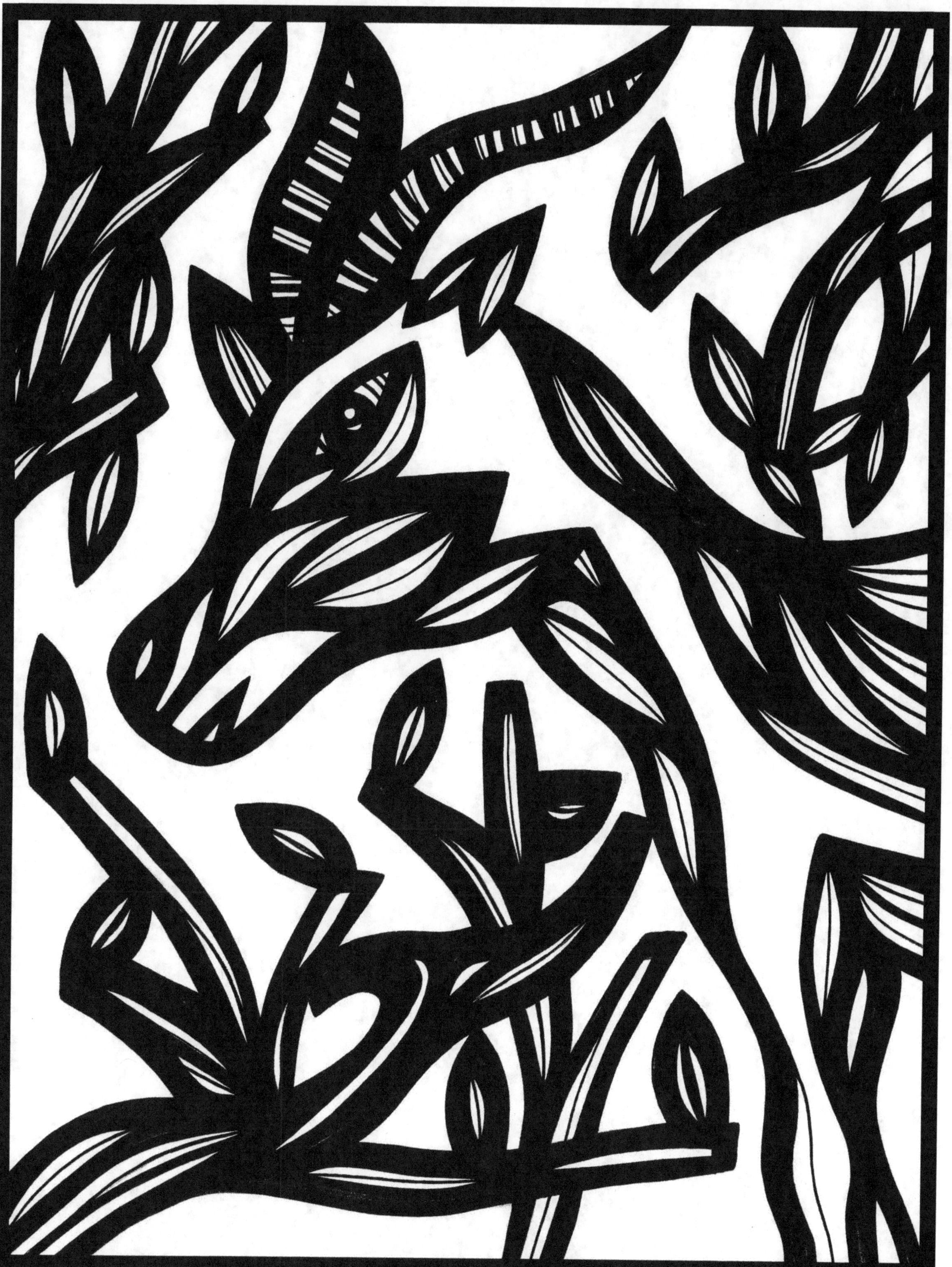

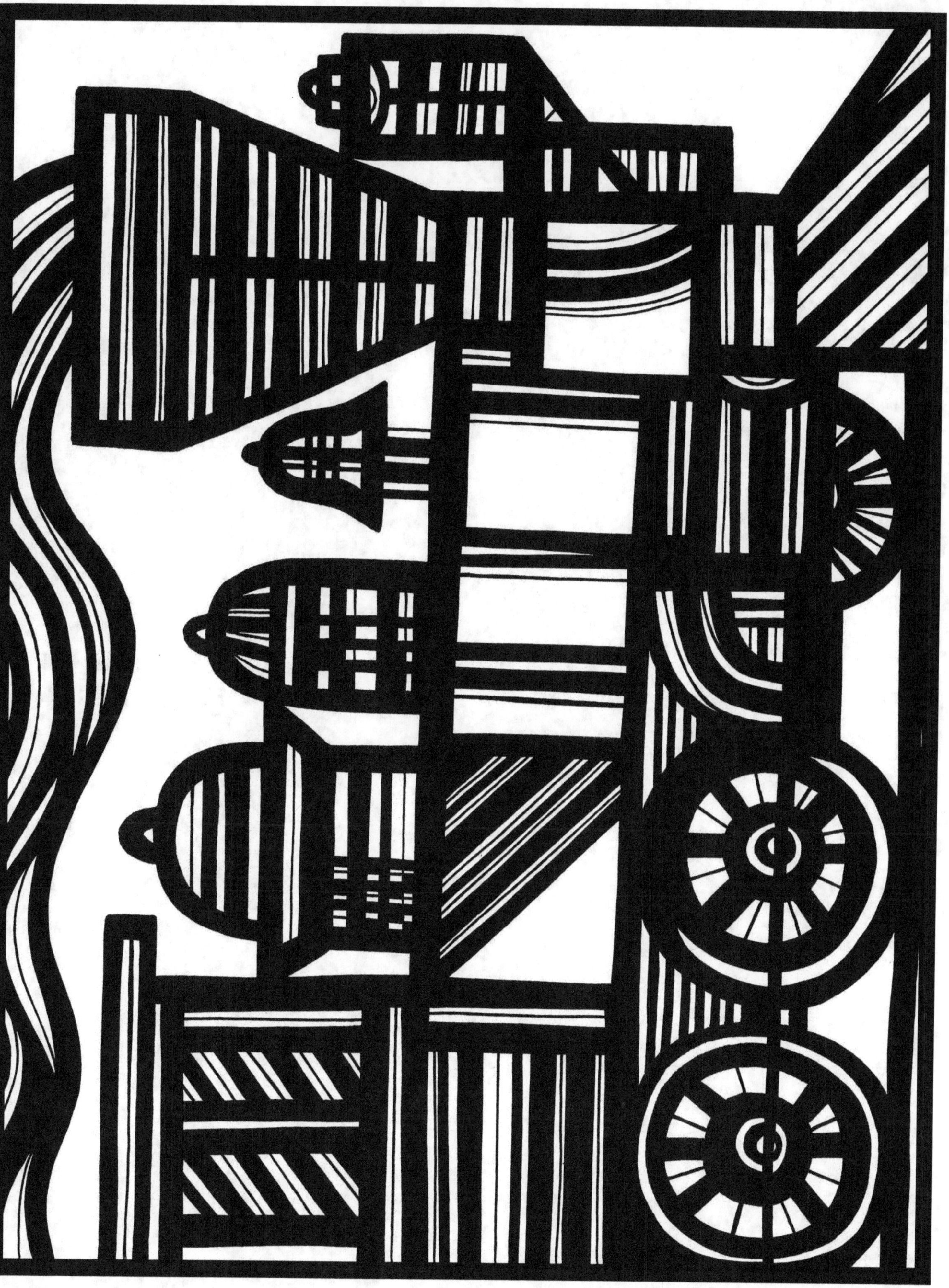

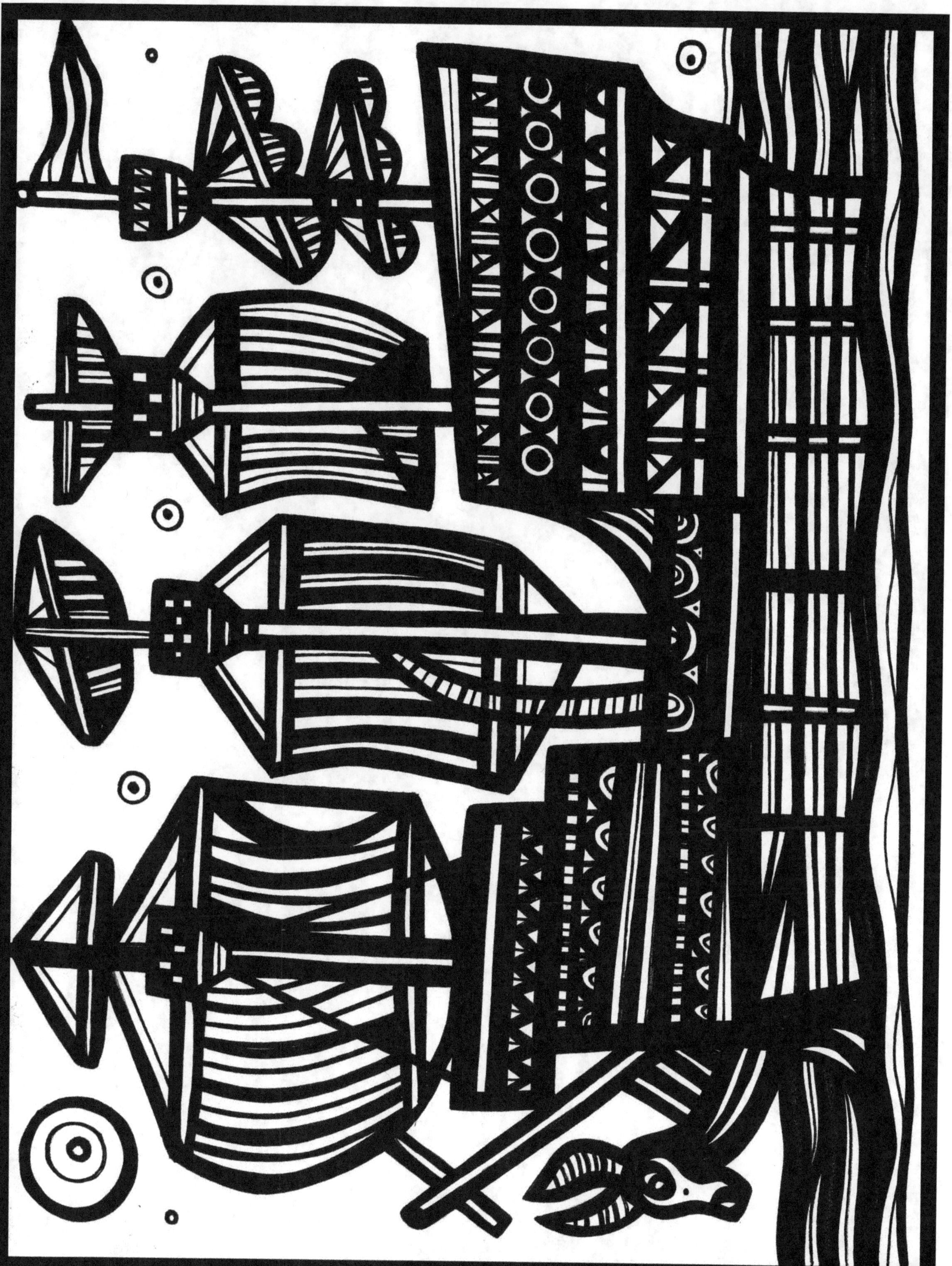

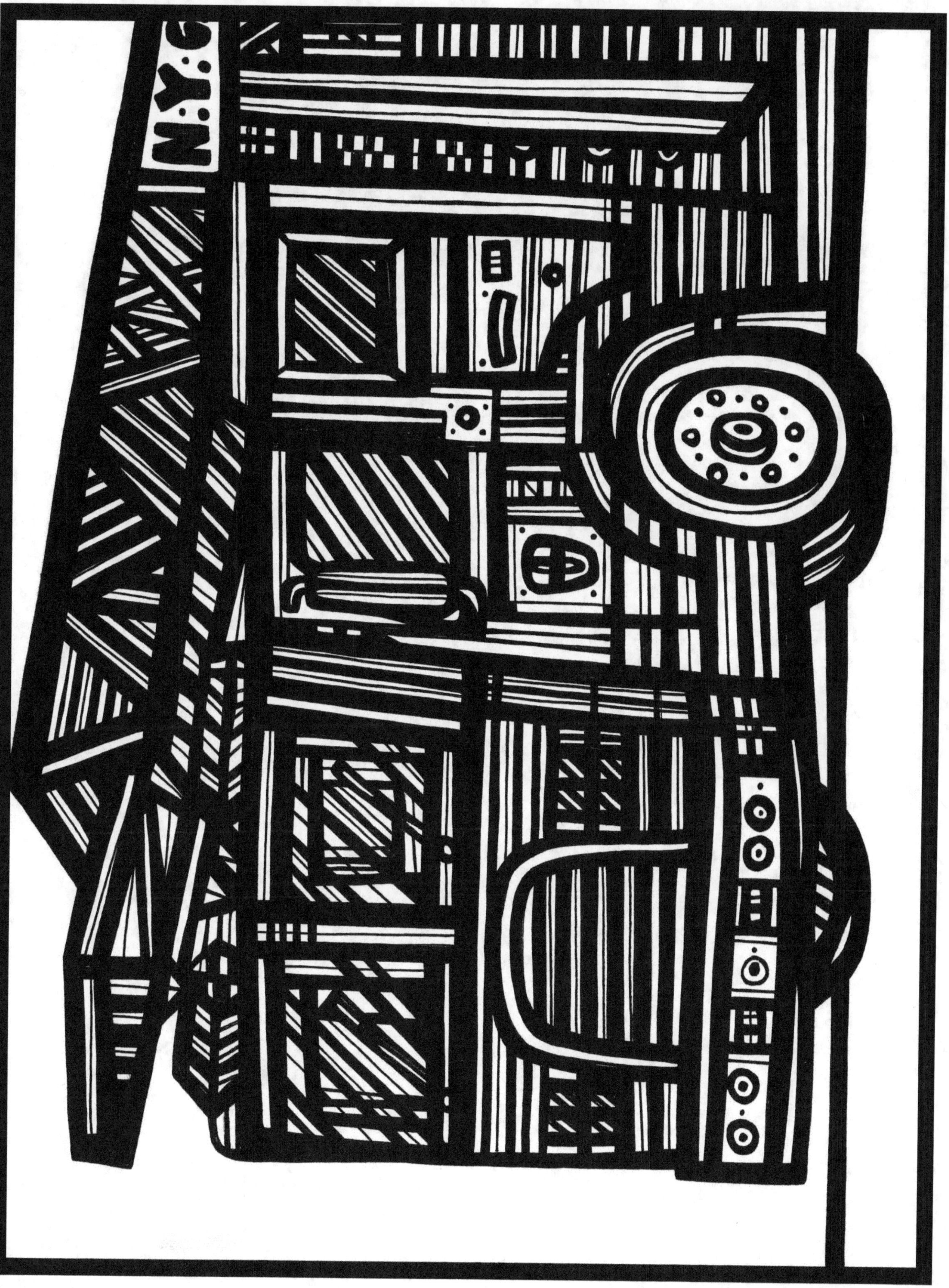

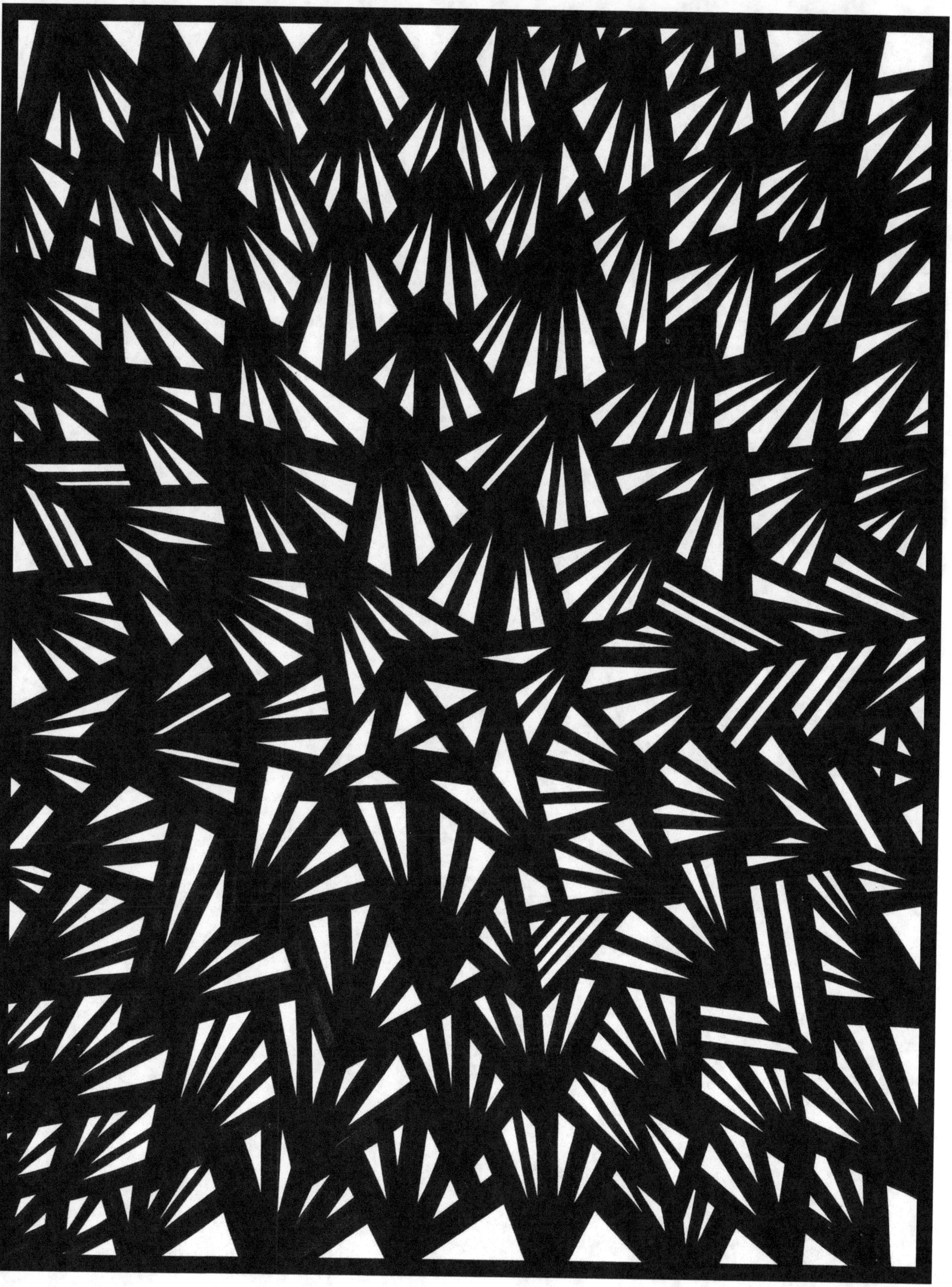

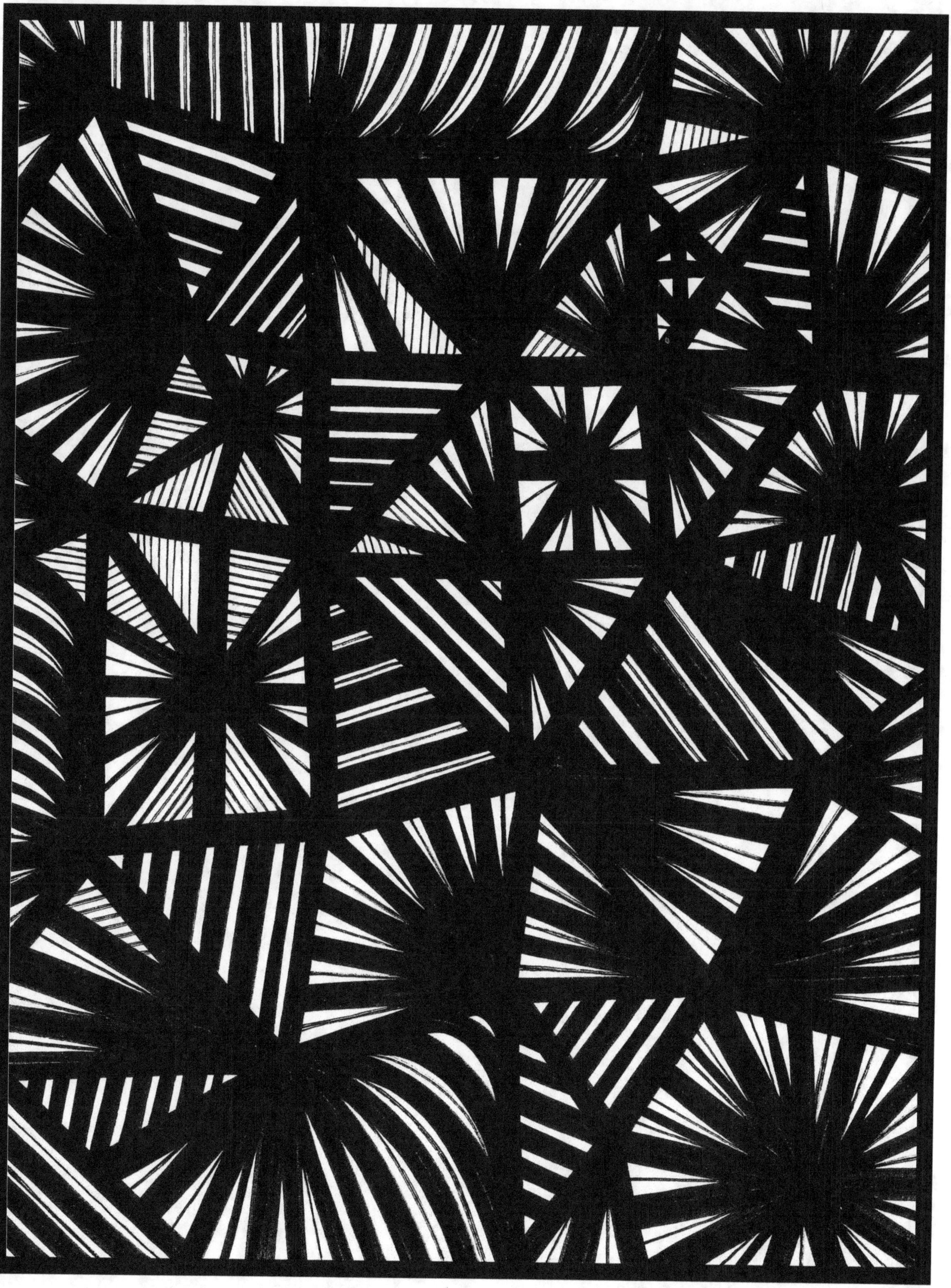

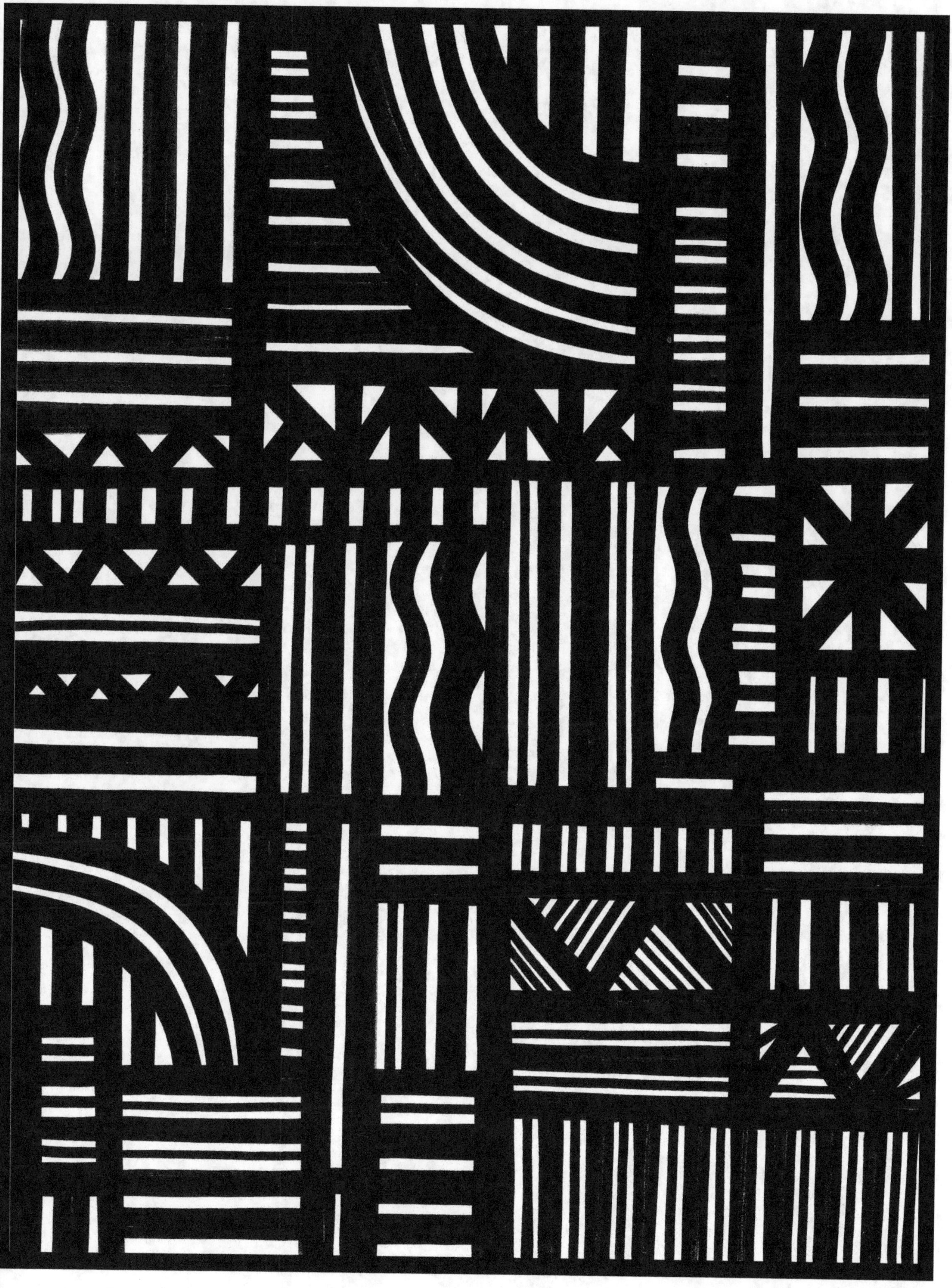

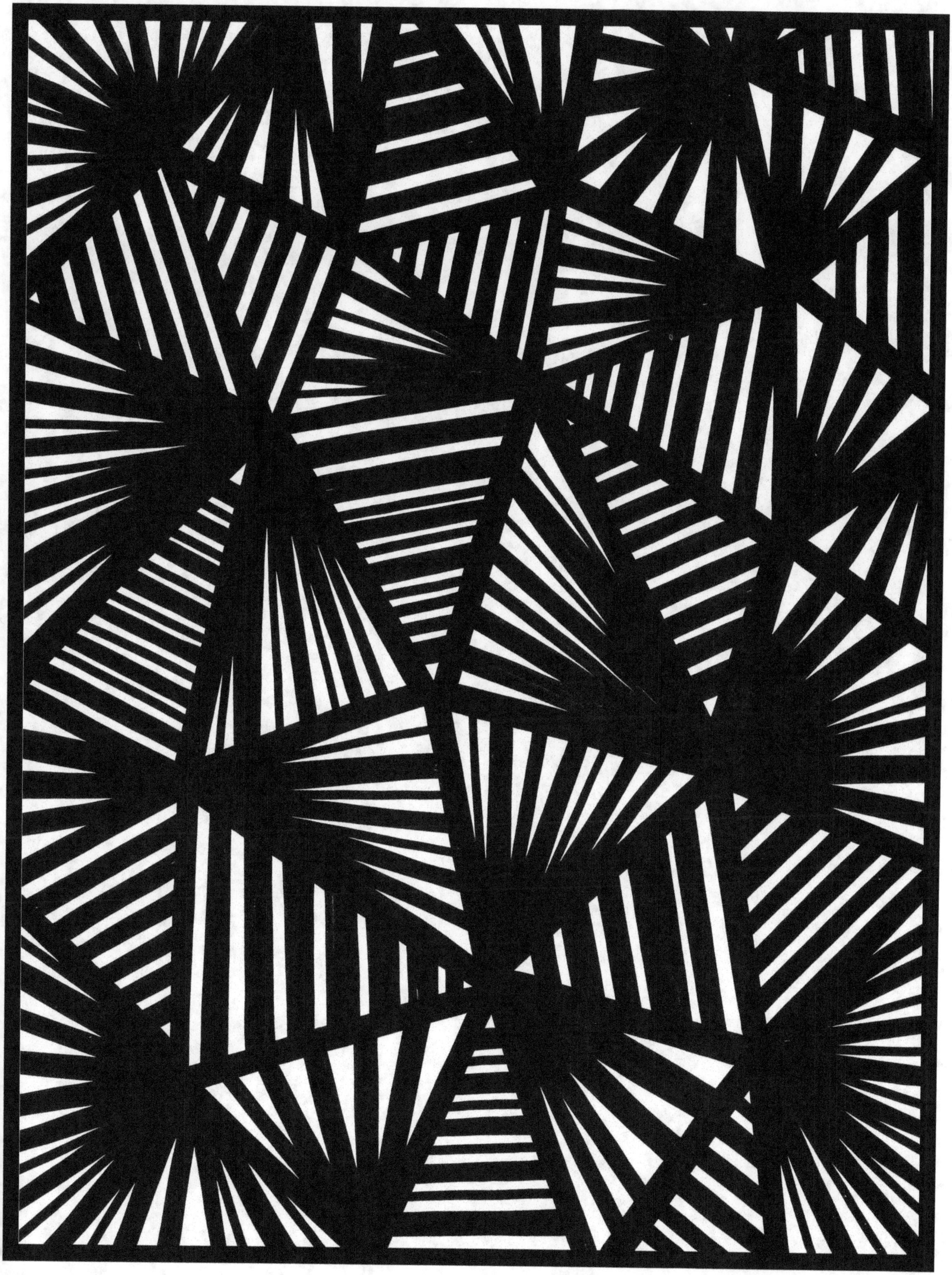

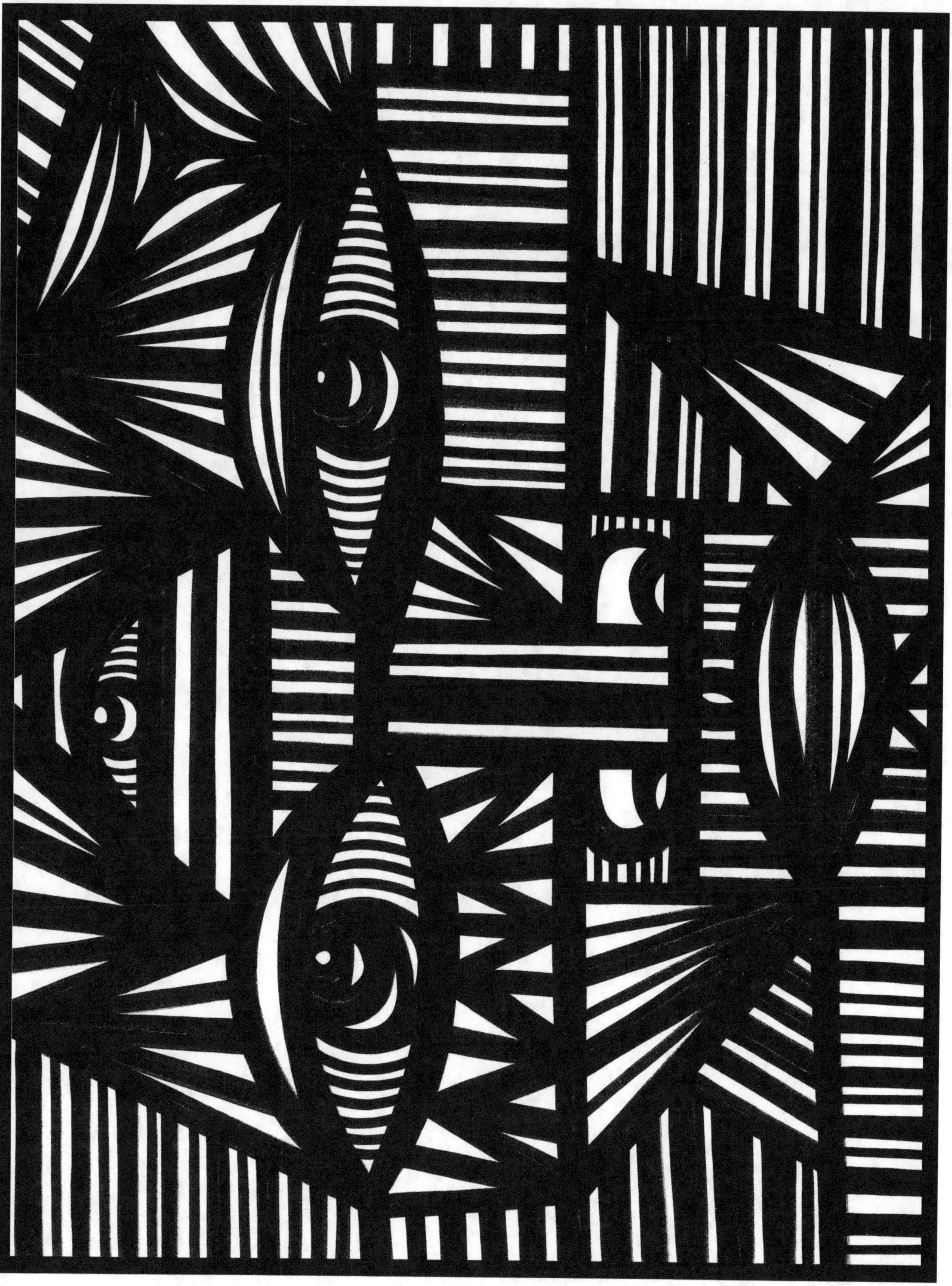

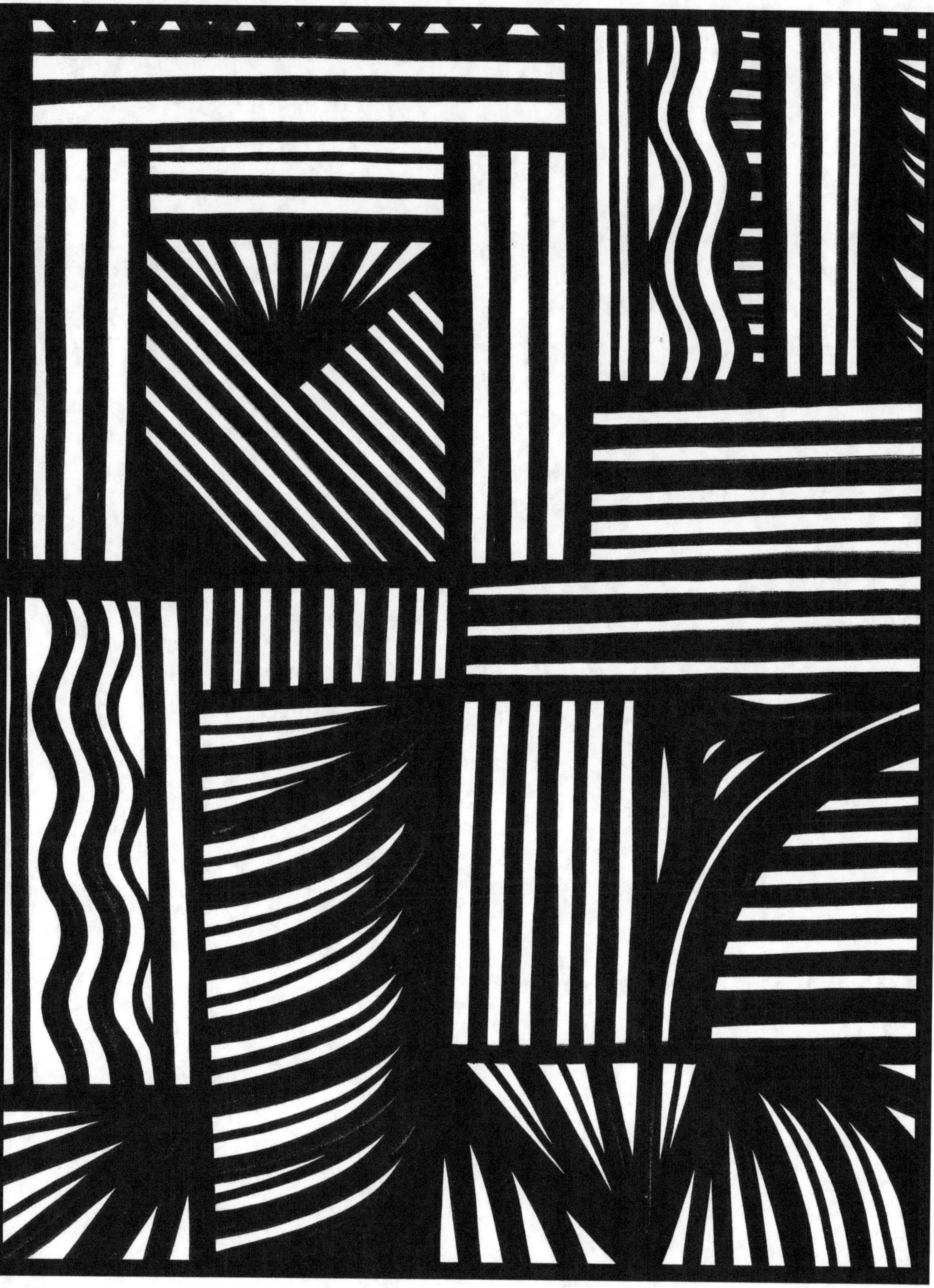

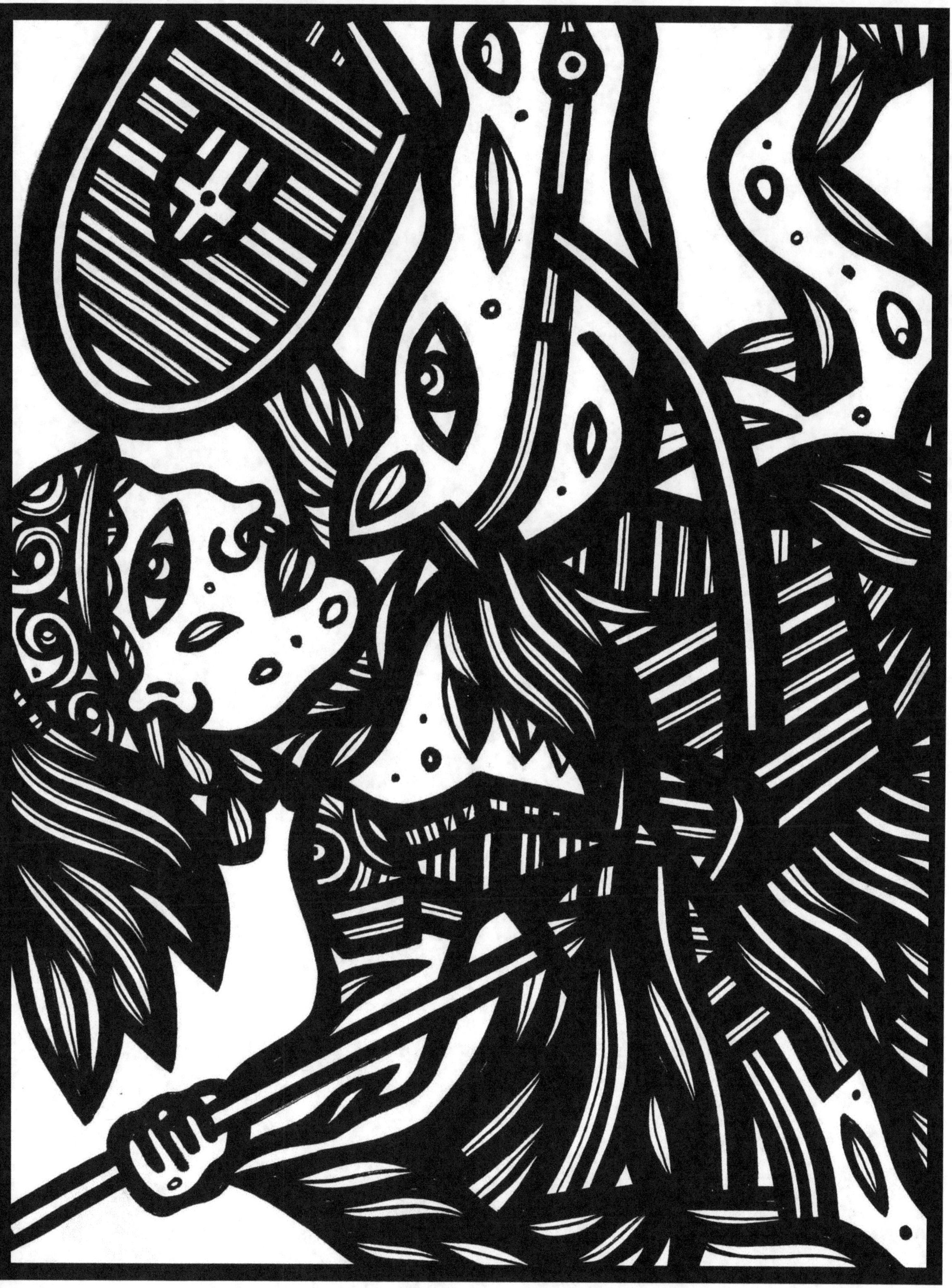

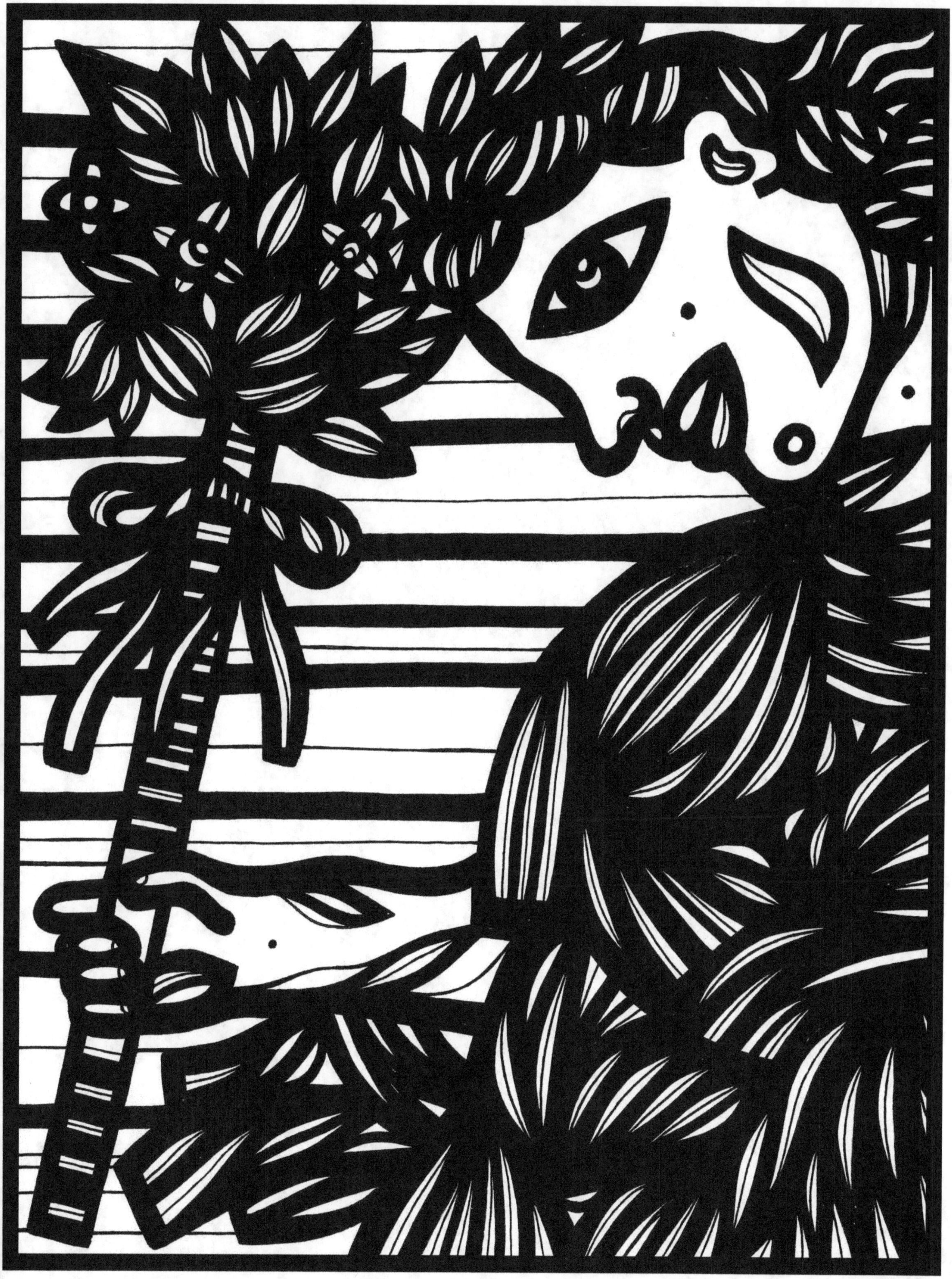

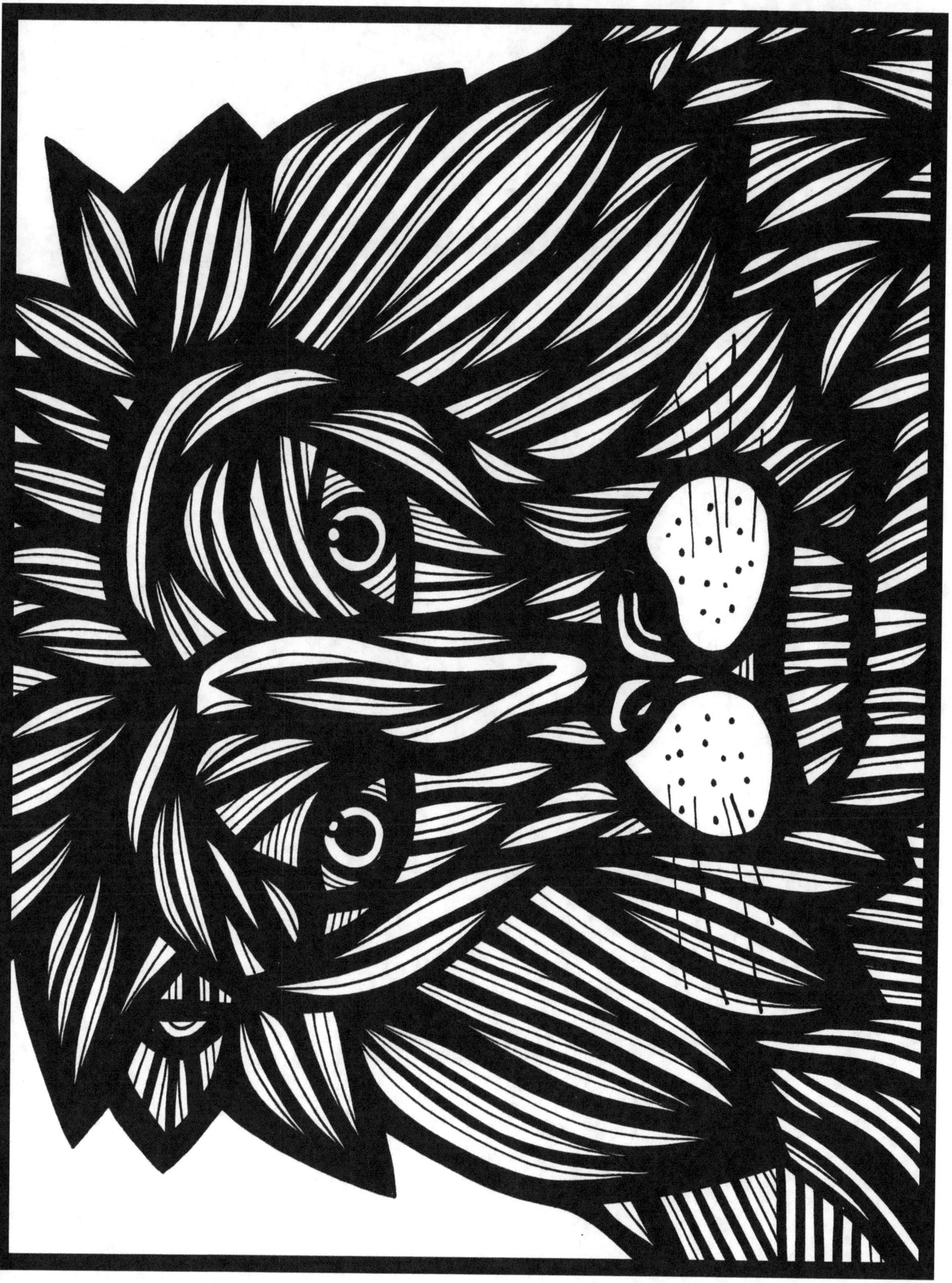

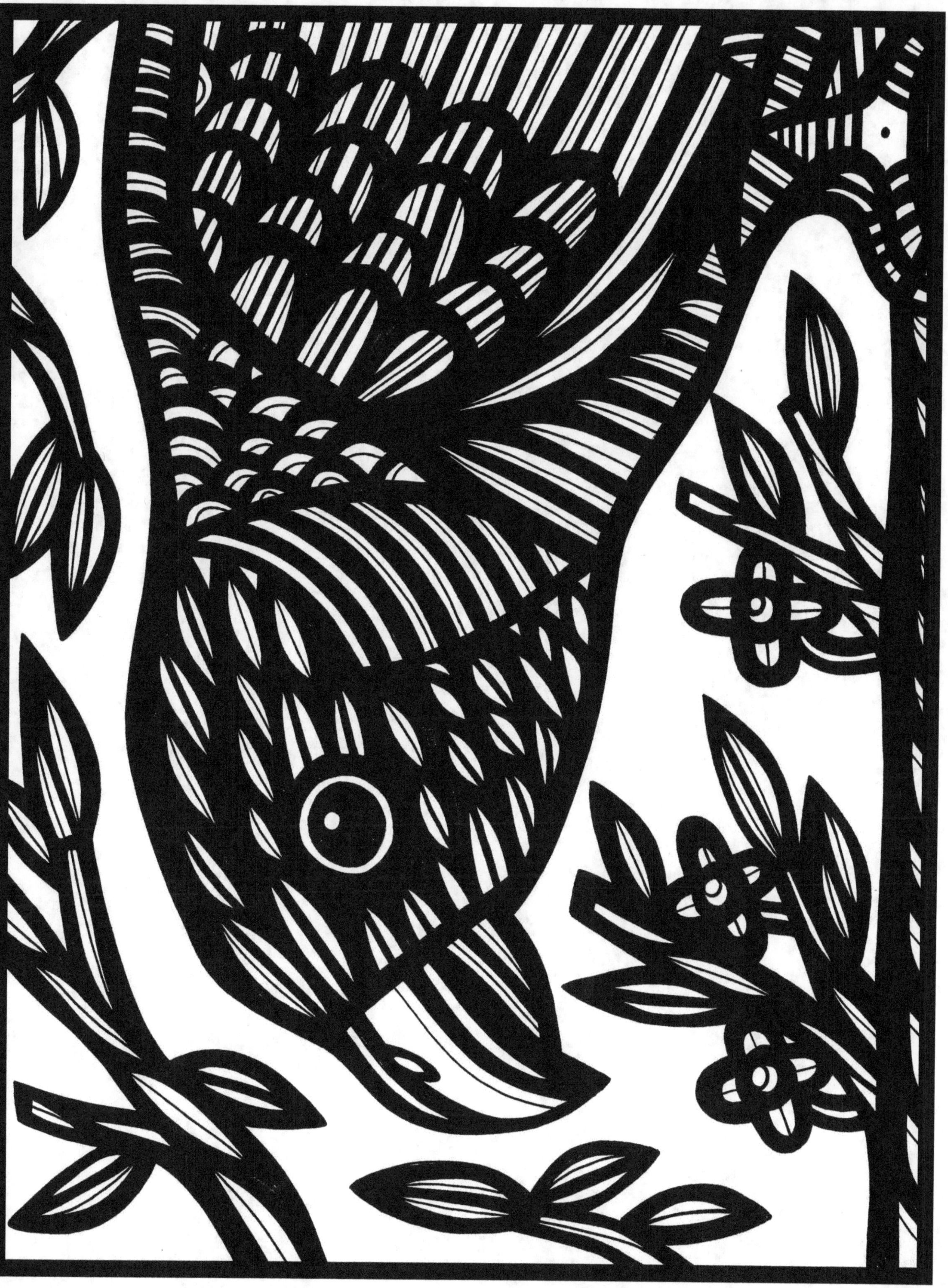

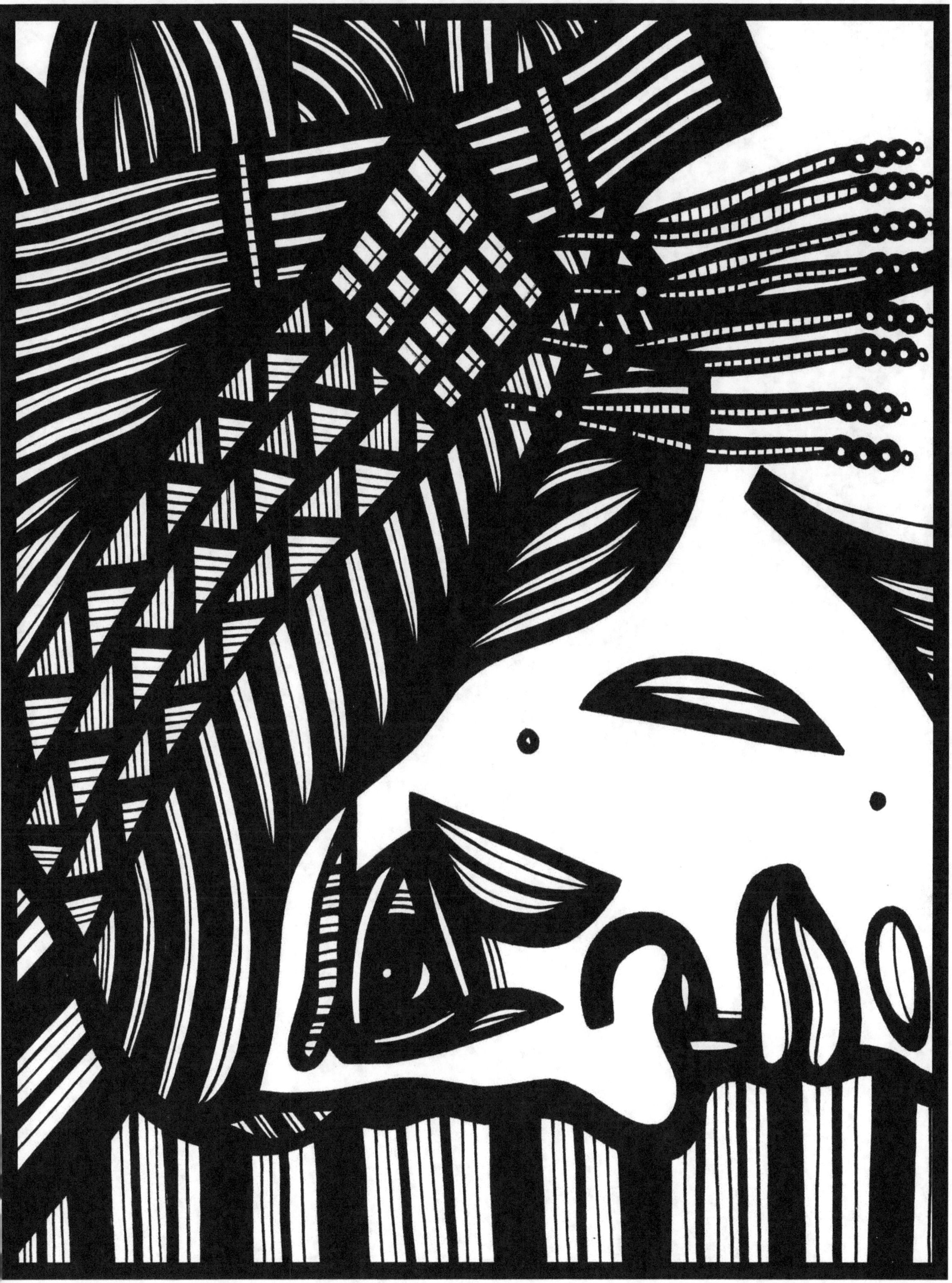

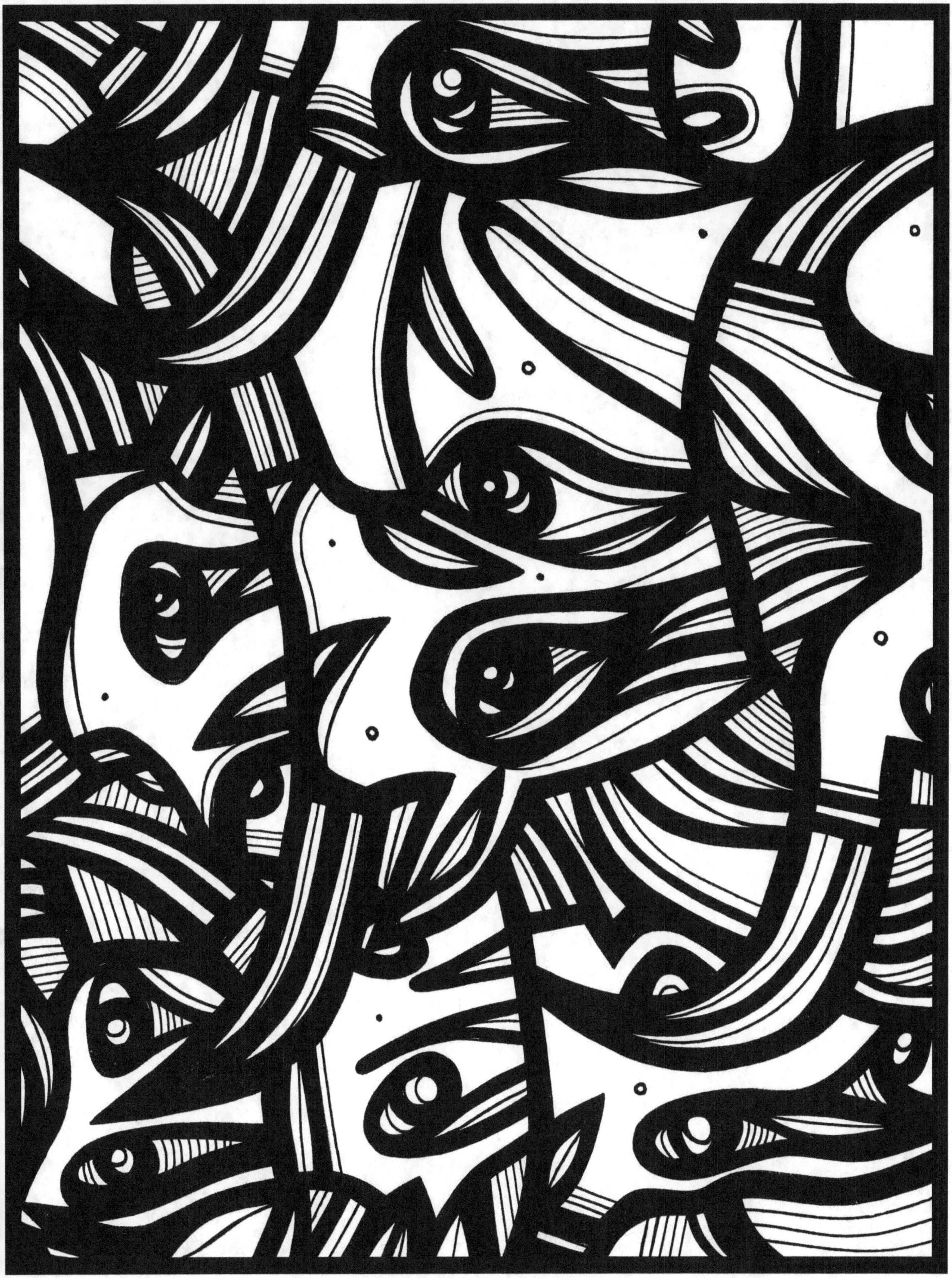

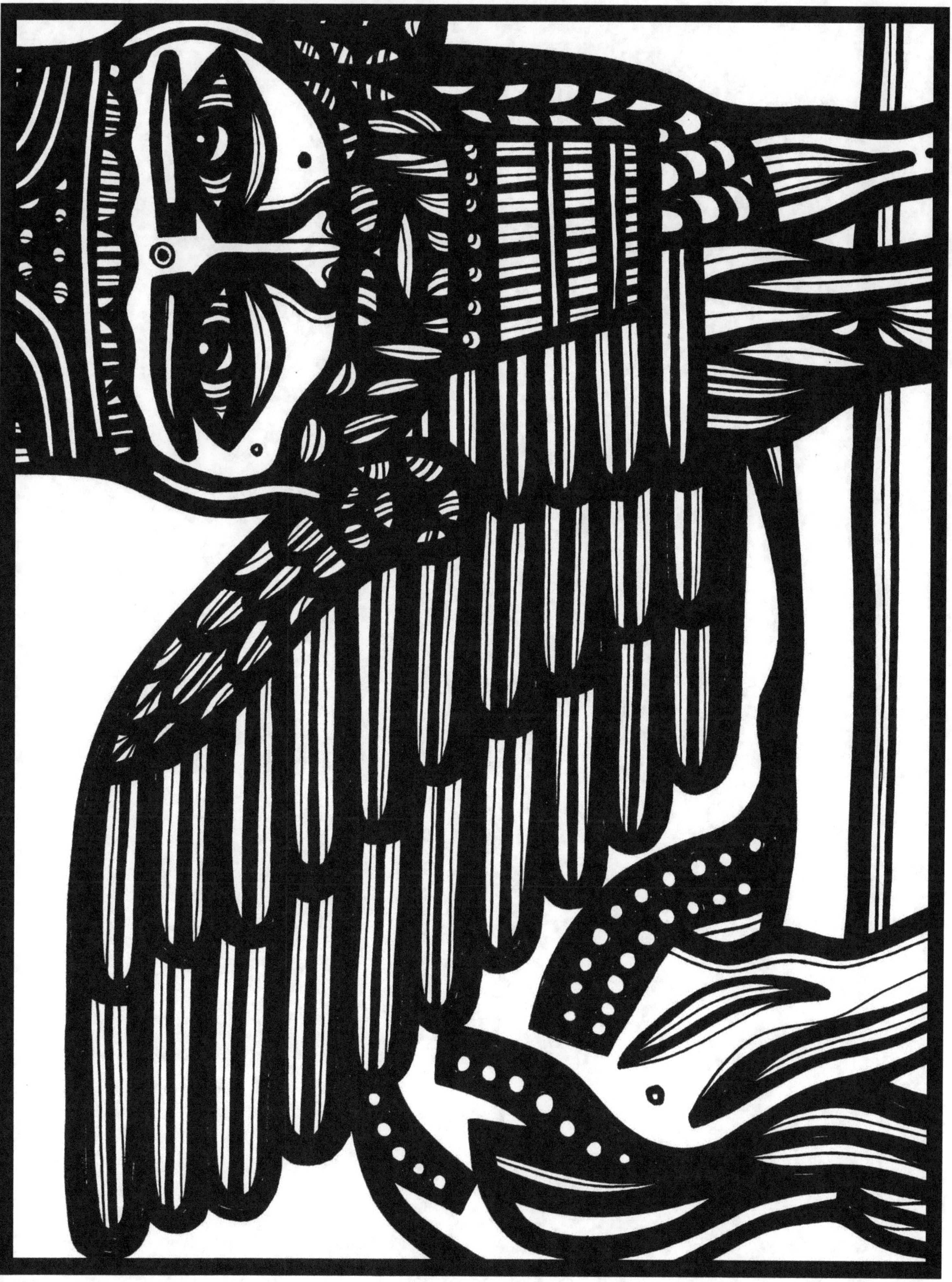

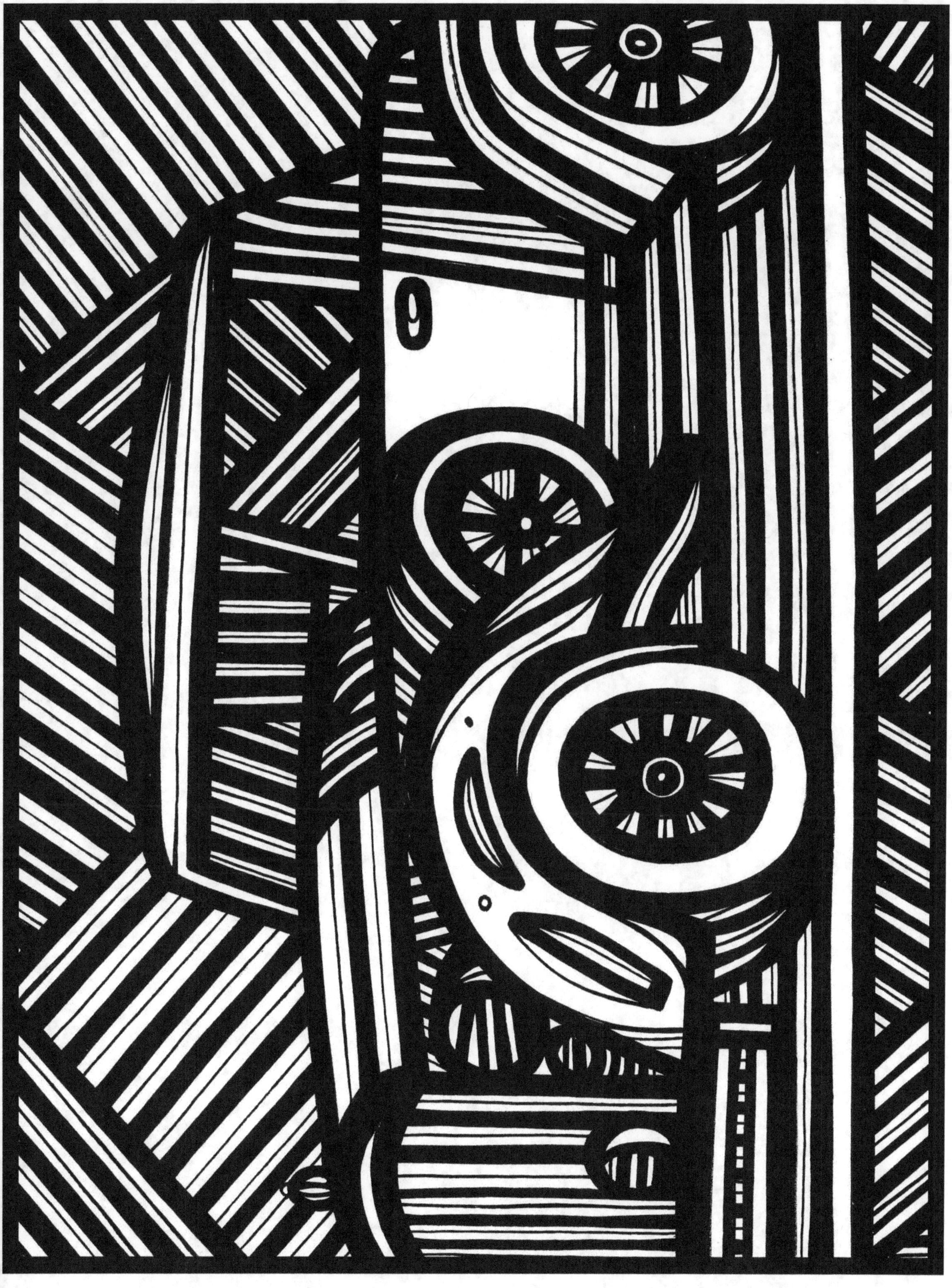
9

THE END, THANK YOU.

MORE BOOKS:
631ART.COM

www.ingramcontent.com/pod-product-compliance
Lightning Source LLC
Chambersburg PA
CBHW080131240526
45468CB00009BA/2362
* 9 7 8 1 7 9 5 6 8 0 9 8 1 *